D1326503

THE
WORLD
WAR II
Album

THE
WORLD
WAR II
Album
BISON GROUP

First published in 1991 by
Bison Books Ltd
Kimbolton House
117A Fulham Road
London SW3 6RL

ISBN 0-86124-876-7

Printed in China

Reprinted 1994

Page 1: A heavily-armed German soldier shows the strain of combat operations.

Pages 2-3: Sherman tanks of the US 7th Armored Division near St Vith early in 1945 shortly after the Battle of the Bulge.

This page: A British A9 cruiser tank in the Egyptian desert in the summer of 1940.

CONTENTS

INTRODUCTION

Introductions usually begin at the beginning of their subject but to do this for World War II would not only be to ignore many of the beneficial insights that can come from hindsight but also to underplay the vast scale of the suffering which the war brought.

This introduction therefore begins with the casualties. Approximately 55 million people died because of the war. Approximately 55 million because nobody knows the true and exact number. Such a massive figure is also difficult to grasp in any meaningful way – it is roughly the total population, men, women and children, of Great Britain. It is worth remembering, too, that each soldier or civilian was someone's father or daughter, wife or child or friend, with all the personal tragedy and loss that these descriptions imply. It is perhaps also worth remembering, in an era familiar with reports of the problems of America's Vietnam veterans, that even healthy survivors of war and combat, whether victors or defeated, might find their lives and personalities altered and in many ways diminished in coming to terms with what they had seen and what had been done by them or in their name.

War's massive destruction is not merely confined to its direct attacks on life of course. Near the war's end for example, American bomber forces switched to new lists of potential targets in Japan because their leaders believed there was little left worth bombing in Japan's largest cities. In the western parts of the Soviet Union roughly two thirds of the homes and factories were destroyed by the fighting and passing armies. Even though British home territory had never been occupied or fought over, the economic strains of the war compelled the maintenance of a harsh system of rationing for several years after the war in that country and damage done by German bombs could not be repaired in many places until well into the 1950s.

That one belligerent country, the United States, bucked this trend and finished the war with its people having a higher standard of living than ever before, provides a neat pointer to the political changes that the war brought about. In 1945 only in the Red Army's massive force in eastern Europe was there a significant counterpoise to America's industrial, financial, political and atomic power. The decades of Cold War that followed arose from this division. Other political changes that derived directly from the war were the end of colonial regimes throughout Asia (with troubles that still continue in what was French Indo-China), the communist revolution in China and many more. Less directly, but just as powerfully, can anyone doubt that the politics and problems of the Middle East would be very different if the war's most horrific evil, the Nazi extermination campaign against the Jews, had not occurred?

What were the origins of this war which was to cause such destruction and to change so much more? Thousands of books have been written on this subject but the principal points can be stated very simply. The settlement of World War I, embodied principally in the Treaty of Versailles, was flawed in a variety of ways. Above all it created real grievances in Germany and problems elsewhere that were expertly manipulated by Hitler in his rise to domestic power and in the years of expansion from 1933-39. For Japan, too, the settlement of World War I, in which she was on the victor's side, had been disappointing and the Washington Naval Agreement of 1922 was also unwelcome in the limitations which it imposed. Gradually militarist groups achieved more and more influence within Japan, embroiling the country ever more deeply in Chinese affairs first in the occupation of Manchuria in 1931 and later in the invasion of large parts of China proper in 1937-39.

Japan and Germany were the aggressors but what of the countries that might have opposed them? The United States had decided on isolationist policies at the end of World War I and these were enforced in the 1930s by a series of Neutrality Laws which forbade arms sales and other steps which might draw the country into war. Britain and France had both suffered badly in the First War and were both as a consequence less able and less willing to repeat the experience. It was not too hard, therefore, to see concessions to Hitler as a reasonable way of buying peace. All the western democracies, too, were greatly preoccupied by the economic and social problems of the Great Depression. Still more concerned with its own internal problems, many of them inflicted by Stalin on his own people, was the other great European power, now to be known since its 1917 Revolution as the USSR. In any case the western countries found it more difficult to deal with Russian communists than the Nazis did, as the events of 1939 which brought the outbreak of war would show.

Left: Hitler and other participants in the so-called 'Beer Hall Putsch' of November 1923.

Above right: World War I US veterans hit by the depression demand that the government make promised bonus payments.

Right: Prime Minister Chamberlain's return from Munich with his worthless peace agreement with Hitler, September 1938.

Previous page: Chancellor Hitler addresses a Nazi meeting.

Das ist ihre Menschenwürde!

1939–40

From the early months of 1939 it was obvious that Hitler's next foreign policy objective was to make gains at Poland's expense. Britain and France had given security guarantees to Poland and belatedly but half-heartedly began negotiations for some form of alliance with the Soviets. Instead the world was surprised on 24 August when the arch-enemies of Communism and Nazism signed a Soviet-German Non-Aggression Pact in Moscow. This pact, agreed by both Hitler and Stalin purely as a matter of expediency, secretly provided for the two to divide Poland between them and this Hitler proceeded to begin after a week of hesitation and last ditch diplomacy. On 1 September 1939 German forces invaded Poland. Britain and France declared war on Germany on the 3rd with Australia and New Zealand joining Britain the same day and Canada and South Africa within the week. World War II in Europe had begun. It should not be forgotten, however, that Japan and China were already fighting and that other European countries and the United States remained neutral for the moment.

The fighting in Poland taught the English-speaking world a new word, *Blitzkrieg*, the German expression meaning lightning war, which summed up what seemed to be the new way of warfare employed by the Germans in the campaign, combining the mobility and strength of tank divisions with the moral and physical power of air attacks. Poland was already beaten when the Soviets invaded the eastern half of the country from 17 September. Warsaw surrendered to the Germans on the 27th and almost all fighting was over by the end of the month.

Hitler hoped to turn almost immediately to attack in the West but bad weather and difficulties with the training and equipment of his forces led to postponements into 1940. Britain and France, all too conscious of the real weaknesses of their forces, also preferred to wait. The result was the so-called Phony War or 'Sitzkrieg' which would last until April 1940 in the West.

In the East it was a different matter. Despite their recent pact, Stalin wished to strengthen the Soviet Union against a possible German attack. In October 1939 he therefore forced the Baltic nations of Estonia, Latvia and Lithuania to concede 'mutual assistance' agreements and would go on to annex them as republics within the USSR in July 1940. In October and November 1939 the Soviets also demanded border concessions from Finland and when these were not forthcoming they attacked. To universal amazement the Finns beat back all the early Soviet attacks despite the huge Soviet numerical advantage but by January the Soviets were beginning to make better use of their superior resources. The Finns made peace and ceded border territory in March and Hitler noted for the future what he thought was the weakness of the Red Army.

The Winter War had drawn attention north to Scandinavia. Britain and France had decided to send help to Finland (via neutral Norway) just before the Finns gave in but the real motive was to cut off the substantial part of Germany's supply of iron ore which came from northern Sweden nearby and was usually shipped via Norwegian ports. These plans were continued despite the Finnish surrender and Germany

too was planning its own aggression against Norway (and Denmark en route). In the event the Germans beat the Allies to the punch by a matter of hours when their landings began on 9 April. The early German conquests included the airfields at Oslo and Stavanger. Aircraft were quickly based there and gave the Germans air superiority which in effect decided the campaign. There were various naval battles in addition to the land fighting and the Allies did succeed in establishing a strong force around Narvik in the north but by this time (late May) this was worthless in the light of events in France. The Allies pulled out and the Norwegian exile government ordered its forces to surrender in June.

Hitler and his generals had been unsure of the best plan to use to attack France but in February 1940 new orders were issued for the main attack to be made in the Ardennes area, led by strong tank forces. This was in fact the weakest point in the Allied line. On the ground the Allied forces were as strong as the Germans but were hampered by a command system that was little better than a shambles, by the poor organisation of their tank forces and by the generally inadequate training of their troops. The result, when the Germans attacked from 10 May, was a debacle. Within ten days the Allied armies had been cut in two by the German drive to the coast; a few days more and the British were compelled to evacuate their whole army from Dunkirk, abandoning virtually all its equipment; and in the final phase in June renewed German advances brought a complete French surrender.

Britain now stood alone, the target for German air attack and possibly invasion. The air attacks were held off, but only just, in extensive air battles in August and September and the Germans turned instead to night bombing of Britain's cities. At the same time, too, German U-Boats were beginning to hit hard at the Atlantic convoys vital for Britain's survival. The British victory in the Battle of Britain did ensure that Britain would survive for the moment and that Germany would have to fight a long war for which its economy was ill-prepared.

Although the US still remained neutral, it was clear where American sympathies generally lay. Isolationism was still a strong force, however, especially as it seemed to most good judges that Britain was likely to lose the war whatever America did. Much help was sent to Britain nonetheless and much more was done to prepare for the eventuality of the US itself going to war. Massive increases in military spending were introduced and a draft bill passed into law also. Finally, President Roosevelt became more free to help Britain as he wished with his re-election for an unprecedented third term in November 1940.

By then the war was spreading in other areas also. Mussolini had decided that Italy should join Hitler's march of conquest and had declared war on Britain and France in June. Little fighting followed at first but in November the British hit the Italian fleet at Taranto and in December began an offensive from Egypt into Libya that was quickly successful. By then, too, Italy had attacked Greece in late October, without warning Hitler in advance, and was soon in trouble in that campaign as well.

Left: British anti-aircraft guns fire at German attackers, Cardiff, August 1940.

Right: One of the heroes of the Battle of Britain was the then Squadron Leader Douglas Bader. Bader had been invalided out of the pre-war RAF following a flying accident in which he lost both legs. At the outbreak of war he managed to persuade the authorities to allow him to rejoin and he once again became a highly respected pilot and leader.

Previous page: Hitler and a group of senior officers watch the bombardment of Warsaw. General Rommel is on Hitler's left and to his right are Keitel and Bormann.

Left: German Foreign Minister Joachim von Ribbentrop (right) shakes hands with the smiling Soviet leader Marshal Josef Stalin at the signing of the Nazi-Soviet Pact. Despite the Nazis' and Communists' previous mutual hatred, this measure of expediency was quickly agreed in August 1939.

Right: One of the secret parts of the Nazi-Soviet agreement provided for the Soviets to join in the occupation of Poland which the Germans were shortly to begin. Here German and Soviet soldiers are seen meeting on the border between their respective occupied areas of Poland after the overrunning of the country.

Below: A German supply unit pushes on into Poland in early September 1939 despite a partially-damaged bridge.

Below right: Troops of the Waffen SS advance cautiously in a damaged Polish town in September 1939.

IC-137808

A
OKĘCIE
1071

Left: German tanks and infantry in the outskirts of Warsaw. The heavy air and ground bombardment of the Polish capital helped reinforce many foreign fears of the power of the German war machine.

Below left: Panzer Mk II Ausf A tanks advance along a muddy forest track. These comparatively lightly armed and protected machines formed a considerable proportion of German tank strength in 1939-40.

Above right: During the months of Phony War that followed the Polish battles one of the few forms of activity along the Western Front between France and Germany was the erection of propaganda banners like the one shown here. This proclaims, from the German side of the border, Hitler's alleged ambition to put an end to the traditional hatred between France and Germany.

Right: Finnish troops in action against Russian attackers during the Russo-Finnish War in the winter of 1939-40. The initial success of the Finns in holding off the much larger Soviet forces attracted much admiration.

Below: Eventually, however, the Finnish defenses were to be overrun, despite the efforts of their troops. Here a Russian unit advances past some antitank obstacles.

Although the European War began in 1939, war between China and Japan had been being waged at high intensity since 1937 with much Chinese territory being overrun by the Japanese. Brutality and atrocities were a common feature of the campaign as the picture, *left*, of harshly treated prisoners awaiting execution, shows.

Right: Japanese troops set up an antiaircraft machine gun.

Below: An infantry attack begins.

Both sides scored a number of notable successes during the period of the Phony War.

Opposite, top two: Kapitänleutnant Gunther Prien took his *U.47* into the main British fleet anchorage at Scapa Flow in the Orkney Islands off northern Scotland on the night of 14 October 1939 and sank the old battleship *Royal Oak*.

Above: A U-Boat gun crew on a training voyage.

Below: The *Admiral Graf Spee* burns after being scuttled by her crew outside Montevideo harbor on 17 December 1939.

Right: The German heavy cruiser *Admiral Hipper*. Armed with eight 8-inch guns and displacing some 14,000 tons, the *Hipper* was a formidable vessel but had a comparatively short range and was often troubled by unreliable engines.

Below right: The *Admiral Graf Spee* pictured shortly before the war. Sent secretly to sea a few days before the outbreak of war, the *Graf Spee* sank a number of Allied ships before being cornered in the River Plate.

Below: The British aircraft carrier *Ark Royal* became one of the most famous ships of the early years of the war particularly because German propaganda radio broadcasts made numerous false claims that she had been sunk.

Right: 8 April 1940, the sinking British destroyer *Glowworm* is photographed off Trondheim fjord, Norway, through the gunsight of the German cruiser *Hipper. Glowworm* had unexpectedly encountered part of the German invasion force bound for Narvik in north Norway.

Below: Vidkung Quisling (right), leader of the Norwegian Nazi Party, the *Nasjonal Samlung*, whose collaborationist activities during the German occupation of his country were to give the English language a new word for traitorous conduct.

Bottom: British troops on a Norwegian quayside during the brief campaign.

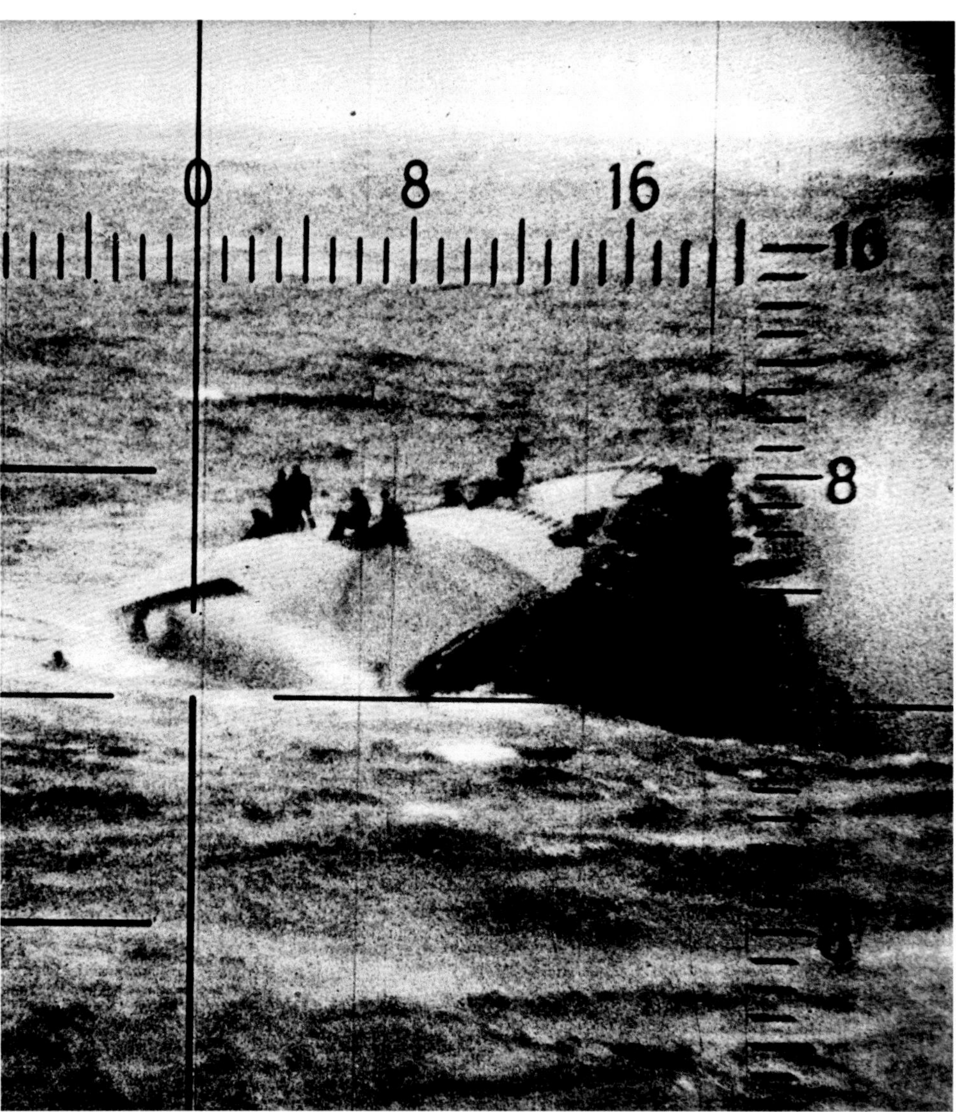

Left: German troops advance into Denmark, 9 April 1940. Neutral Denmark was overrun in a matter of hours, simultaneously with the opening of the German invasion of Norway.

Right: Some of the fiercest fighting of the Norwegian campaign was around the port of Narvik where this group of German soldiers is shown.

Far right: German troops on the advance during the Norwegian campaign.

Below: German troops board their Junkers transport aircraft ready to set out for Norway. German airborne forces seized vital airfields in southern Norway in the first hours of their attack and this resource gave their side the vital advantage of command of the air for the remainder of the campaign.

Left: German infantrymen study their map during training for the invasion of France.

Right: Dutch troops patrol one of their country's dykes.

Far right: Men of an SS unit in action with their machine gun. Comparatively few Waffen SS troops fought in France in 1940.

Below right: The classic image of the *Blitzkrieg*, the diving Stuka. The Ju-87 did indeed play an important part in supporting the advancing German tank forces and creating the demoralisation among the Allied troops which made the German victory possible.

Below: German heavy artillery in action during the fighting in France in 1940.

Above: Abandoned equipment and sunken ships in the harbor at Dunkirk after the end of the evacuation of the British forces attest to the violence of the fighting and the scale of the British and French defeat.

Below: Although in reality the largest numbers of troops were saved by the Royal Navy and the larger civilian vessels, as this picture shows the little ships of the Dunkirk legend also played a notable part.

Above: German troops continue their advance despite demolitions.

Above right: British troops being evacuated from Dunkirk come aboard the old destroyer *Vanquisher* in Dunkirk harbor.

Above left: German motorcycle troops pause during their rapid advance.

Above: A well-armed German paratrooper poses for the camera. German airborne forces made important landings in Holland in the early stages of the campaign of 1940 but their most famous achievement was the capture of the Belgian fortress of Eben Emael.

Left: Polish troops, exiled in France after the defeat of their country, parade in the town of Arras.

Right: German propaganda picture of a Panzer Mk IV, the most powerful German tank in service in 1940. This photo is taken from an English language edition of the propaganda magazine *Signal* and the original caption begins with the proud comment 'Knights of our Times . . .'

Right: German troops move into Paris. In the background is the Cathedral of Notre Dame.

Below: A German photograph, taken in the captured port of Calais, of official French notices to the people and to the French and British forces. The notices give directions to stragglers from the British and French armies.

Bottom: Not all the British forces in France were evacuated from Dunkirk. Plans were even made for the British to return to France but these were overtaken by the success of the second phase of the German advance which brought the French capitulation. Here British troops from one of the last fighting formations in France, the 51st (Highland) Division, are captured near St Valery on the Channel coast along with members of various French units.

Left: As the Battle of Britain gets under way the leading German fighter ace Werner Molders describes the maneuvers of a combat to a group of his comrades.

Below: Pilots of the RAF's Number 1 Squadron run to their Hurricane fighter planes. This picture was actually taken at a base in France during the winter of 1939-40 although the Hurricane, of course, was to gain greatest fame in the Battle of Britain. This photograph also illustrates the pace of technical change during the war. Most of the aircraft shown have the 2-bladed propellers with which the Hurricane started the war but which were replaced by the time of the Battle of Britain with the 3-bladed version shown on the second fighter in the line. Among other changes made to the Hurricane during these months was the introduction of metal rather than fabric-covered wings which also aided speed and maneuverability.

Far left: A. G. Lewis, a South African pilot of 85 Squadron, climbs out of his Hurricane after a sortie. Lewis had the distinction of shooting down six enemy aircraft in one day later in September 1940.

Left: Luftwaffe aircrew wait for the order to go into action at their base in northern France. Change the uniforms and the picture could easily be of their opponents 'somewhere in England.'

Right: Assignments are marked up for German bomber forces, as the display shows, on 13 July 1940. In this phase of the Battle of Britain the main air actions were over British shipping convoys in the English Channel.

Below: A formation of Heinkel 111 bombers heads for a British target. First introduced into military service in 1936, even in the improved versions in service in 1940 this aircraft was somewhat outdated with a modest bomb load and being dangerously vulnerable to interception.

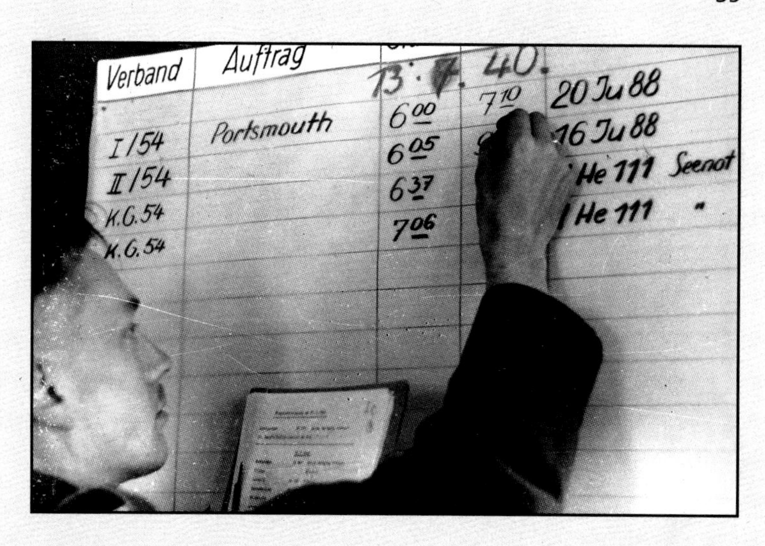

Top left: German Dornier 17 bombers over East London on 7 September 1940.

Above left: Air Marshal Dowding, head of RAF Fighter Command and architect of the British defense system for the Battle of Britain.

Left: Although later historians calmly describe the German decision to attack London as an error, the damage done was nonetheless real and extensive.

Top: One of the fighter control rooms which were the key to the British defense in the Battle of Britain.

Above: Repair and maintenance operations on Messerschmitt 109 fighters.

Right: Although the process was at first officially discouraged by the authorities, London's Tube stations were soon pressed into service as air raid shelters during the night attacks of the Blitz.

2
A L

ZD

Left: A Messerschmitt 110 *Zerstorer* in flight over the English coast. The events of the Battle of Britain quickly proved that these heavy, clumsy, 'destroyer' fighters were of little use in daylight air fighting.

Below left: Flames spurt from the exhaust of a Spitfire's Merlin engine as it starts up. This was in fact a common ocurrence and not an indication of any defect.

Right: A *Schwarm* of Me 109 fighters in flight over the English Channel. During the Battle of Britain some RAF units still employed the closer (and useless) formations that were part of the doctrine of Fighting Area Attacks.

Below right: General Hugo Sperrle commanded Luftflotte III during the Battle of Britain.

Below: General Ernst Udet had been a notable fighter ace during World War I but proved less able as the head of German aircraft production at the start of World War II.

Hoping for a share of what seemed to be Hitler's glorious victory, Mussolini declared war on Britain and France on 10 June 1940. The obvious area for confrontation between British and Italian forces was North Africa.

Right: A British Mk VI light tank demonstrates its ability to breach wire defenses during a desert exercise in May 1940.

Far right: One of the many respects in which the Italian forces were poorly prepared for war was in their continued retention of biplane fighter aircraft in front line service not merely in 1940 but even as late as 1942. These are pictured in Sicily in that year.

Opposite page, center left: Officers of the 11th Hussars enjoy a comfortable break during patrol operations on the Egypt-Libya border in July 1940.

Opposite page, center right: The British Commander-in-Chief, Middle East, from the beginning of the war until July 1941 was General Wavell (left). An imaginative and talented soldier, among his unusual accomplishments for a general was his editorship of a well-known anthology of poetry. With Wavell in this photograph taken in April 1941 is General Charles de Gaulle, leader of the Free French.

Below: British armored cars on patrol in the desert.

20
20

1941

1941 was the year in which World War II truly became a global conflict.

This transformation was made by two devastating surprise attacks – Germany's advance into the Soviet Union and Japan's 'day of infamy' at Pearl Harbor – that were astonishing tactical successes and yet, as time would prove, dreadful strategic blunders. Perhaps the best summary of the difference between the position at the start and end of 1941 was Winston Churchill's. Before Pearl Harbor, he recalled, it was difficult to see how the war could be won. After Pearl Harbor, with US industrial and financial power enlisted on the Allied side, victory was certain, whatever difficulties lay ahead, merely a matter 'of the proper application of overwhelming force.'

Even before the first of these two transforming events, the opening of Hitler's Operation Barbarossa, there had been numerous developments in what was clearly a widening war.

President Roosevelt had set the tone of US policy for the coming year in one of his famous 'fireside chat' radio broadcasts on 29 December 1940 when he spoke of his plan to make the US into the 'arsenal of democracy'. A few days later he spoke of the 'four freedoms' which America was determined to preserve: the freedom of speech and of worship and from fear and want. The first and crucial step to put these policies into operation was the Lend-Lease Act which passed Congress in March. Essentially this meant that Britain, despite having exhausted all its foreign reserves and securities, could continue to order war materials and other supplies from the US while only expecting to pay for them after the war. After the German invasion of the USSR, Lend-Lease aid was extended to the Soviets and in due course every other Allied nation also benefited. Churchill had asked Americans 'Give us the tools and we will finish the job' but in fact the US was already doing more than this. From the middle of the year US warships were escorting many merchant convoys, including British vessels, more or less half way across the Atlantic and, as incidents in September and October involving the US destroyers *Kearny* and *Reuben James* showed, America was already involved in a shooting war – neutral or not.

The British and Americans had held secret military talks in the early weeks of 1941 and had agreed, among other things, that, if America became involved in war against Germany and Japan, defeating Germany would be given the higher priority. As the year progressed, war with Japan did indeed become more likely. Then as now, Japan was dependent on imports of oil and other raw materials. In July a new Japanese government demanded and took military bases in French Indo-China. The US, Britain and the exile Dutch government immediately retaliated by freezing Japanese assets and halting oil and other exports to Japan from the Dutch East Indies, Malaya and other areas. Seventy five percent of Japan's foreign trade and 90 percent of her oil sup-

plies were cut off. Various series of peace talks to settle Pacific and Chinese problems followed but these failed. Faced with a choice of giving in or going to war before reserves ran out, Japan chose war.

In the battles already taking place in Europe the Germans bailed their Italian ally out of trouble in Greece, overrunning that country and Yugoslavia in April-May and sent sufficient forces to north Africa to ensure a year of fluctuating fortunes in that campaign. The events of the European war were dominated, however, by the German attack on the USSR which began on 22 June. The German panzers struck hundreds of miles into Russia and captured hundreds of thousands of prisoners in repeated encirclement operations through the summer and fall. Paradoxically, despite these successes, it was the Germans who were becoming worn out by the losses of the campaign and the Russians who were assembling new reserves. In early December the Germans were stumbling to a halt in bitter winter weather literally in sight of Moscow when the Soviet reserves attacked and threw them back. Within a few days Hitler took two decisions that were effectively to establish the course of the remainder of the war. He sacked his Army Commander in Chief to take more direct personal control of the fighting on the Eastern Front and, in the aftermath of Pearl Harbor, he declared war on America. There had until then been no certainty that the US would fight in Europe but now Hitler had ensured that Germany would definitely lose the war.

Above: A notice gives rules for the bypass road built around Tobruk during its long siege by the Germans and Italians in North Africa. As the notice shows, the road was named 'Axis Street'.

Left: Soviet troops training with antitank rifles. These weapons were in service with most armies at the beginning of the war but improvements in tank armor soon left them outdated.

Right: Hitler studies a map of the Russian fighting with, left, Keitel, the Chief of Staff at Armed Forces High Command, and Brauchitsch, the Army Commander in Chief.

Previous page: Devastation in the aftermath of the Japanese attack on Pearl Harbor.

Left: One form of indoor air-raid shelter being demonstrated for the camera.

Right: Britain was quick to take steps to mobilise women for new jobs in wartime. Here members of the Auxiliary Territorial Service operate Kine Theodolite equipment at an anti-aircraft site.

Far right: A German bomber crew prepares for their night flight to England.

Below: A second photograph of ATS members at work on an antiaircraft site. Here they are operating the height finding equipment.

Below right: Rudimentary facilities in a large air raid shelter in south-east London.

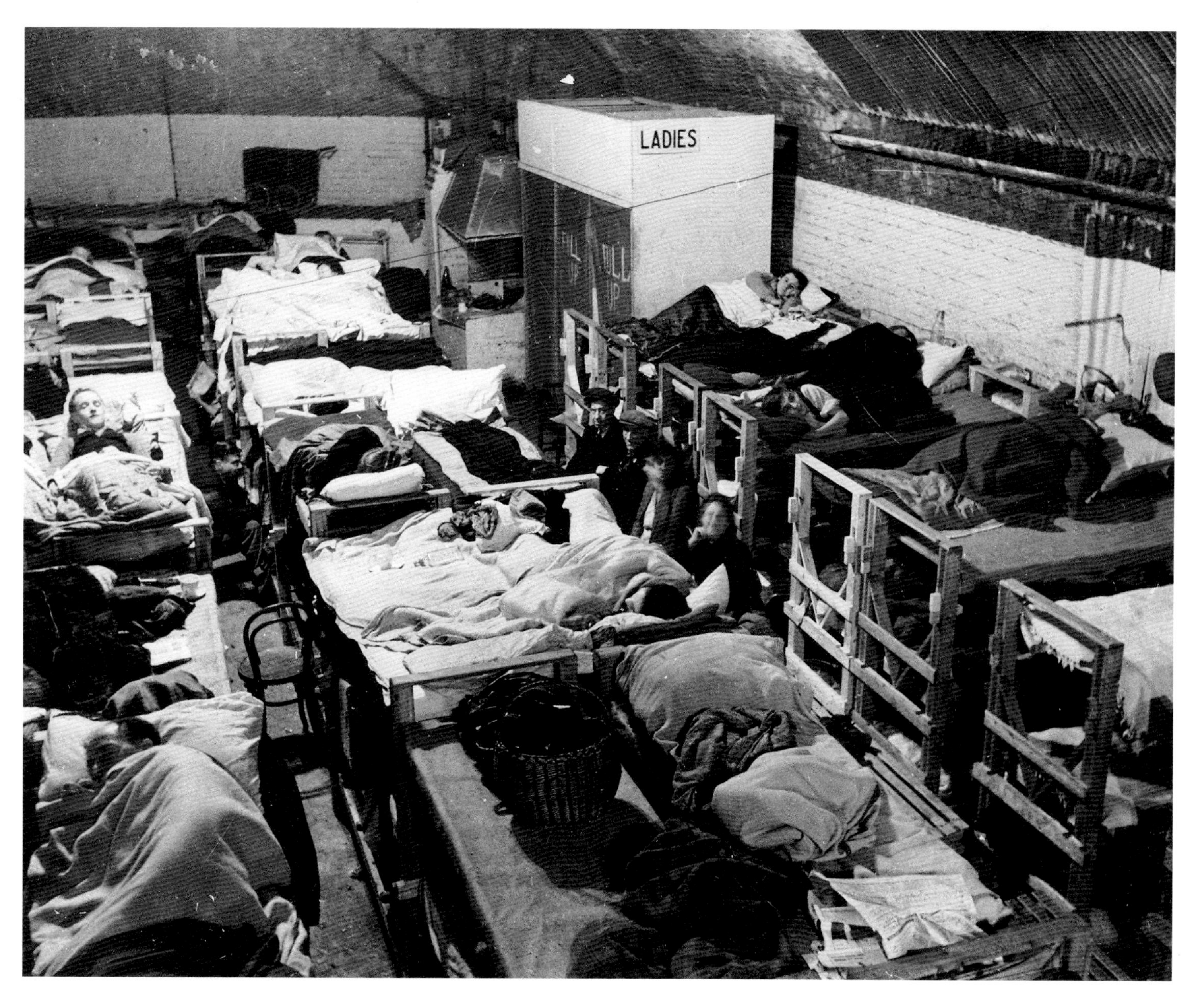
LADIES

ACHILLION

Above left: German troops round up prisoners during their rapid conquest of Greece and Yugoslavia in April 1941.

Above: At the conclusion of the campaign German soldiers and airmen enjoy a visit to the Parthenon in Athens.

Left: British troops pass through a Greek village early in 1941. British troops were sent to Greece to help the Greeks in their fight against the Italian forces invading from Albania but could put up little effective resistance when the Germans intervened.

Right: A motley collection of Yugoslavian soldiers. Although the Yugoslav Army did almost nothing to prevent the German invasion, for much of the rest of the war the country was the scene of considerable and fierce fighting both against the Germans and between different Yugoslav factions. Eventually the Communist Partisan forces, led by Marshal Tito, would triumph.

D

Far left: Admiral Horthy was Hungary's leader for much of the war. He sent forces to join Hitler's invasions of Yugoslavia and the USSR but does not seem to have been at all wholehearted in his support for Germany.

Left: German Mk III assault gun in the streets of Athens. The StuG III was one of the most important weapons in the German arsenal in 1941 but Hitler had made the administrative error of assigning the assault gun force and its technical development to the artillery rather than the tank arm which led to poor control over designs and production priorities.

Above: The scene at Maleme airfield, Crete, 21 May 1941. Burning Ju-52 transports show the ferocity of the battle for the airfield but, once the New Zealand defenders had been pushed back, the Germans were able to reinforce their troops on Crete and the battle could only have one result.

Below: German paratroops on the attack on Crete. Casualties among the German airborne forces were very high and they were never again used in the airborne role, fighting thereafter as ordinary infantry.

Above left: The German battleship *Bismarck* during gunnery exercises in the Baltic shortly before her Atlantic sortie in May 1941.

Left: The old British aircraft carrier *Argus* sporting an interesting disruptive camouflage pattern.

Above: The Short Sunderland was one of the workhorses of British maritime patrol operations. This example seems to be in flight over a troop convoy composed of several large passenger ships and with a battleship leading the center column.

Right: Admiral Sir John Tovey commanded Britain's Home Fleet, 1940-43. He is pictured here on his flagship, the battleship *King George V*, aboard which he led the action which sank the *Bismarck*.

Below: Britain had taken control of Iceland in May 1940 to establish bases to protect the shipping routes. During 1941 the US began to support Britain more openly and in July 1941 the British garrison on Iceland was replaced by an American force. Here British Prime Minister Churchill takes the salute of a US Marine parade on the island during a visit in August 1941.

Top: Lookouts aboard *U.86* search for Allied convoys. Both the German submarine strength and the Allied escort forces were greatly expanded during 1941.

Above: One aspect of US aid to Britain during 1941, before the US was at war with Germany, was the creation and patrolling of 'neutrality zones' in the western Atlantic. The *Mahan* Class destroyer *Drayton* is seen during one such operation.

Right: The conquest of France did not only provide the Germans with U-Boat bases convenient for the convoy routes but also air bases as well. A gunner on a Focke-Wulf Kondor aircraft is shown shortly before leaving on an Atlantic mission.

One feature of Hitler's attack on Russia was the employment of troops from an unlikely collection of German allies and friends.

Above: Artillery men adjust shell fuses during operations in support of the Spanish volunteer division on the Eastern Front in the winter of 1941-42.

Right: Finland also joined Germany in the attack on the USSR but the principal intention was to recover territory lost to the Soviets during the Winter War of 1939-40. Finnish troops are shown here ready to attack on the Leningrad front. The soldier in the center seems to be about to fire a rifle grenade.

Above: Field Marshal Fedor von Bock had commanded an Army Group in the conquest of France, and in the attack on the USSR in 1941 he led Army Group Center.

Above left: Barges carry supplies across Lake Ladoga to the besieged city of Leningrad.

Above right: Colonel General Heinz Guderian meets tank crewmen on the Russian front in September 1941.

Below: Italian troops on the retreat during typical winter weather on the Russian Front.

Far left: Mussolini takes the salute at a German and Italian parade.

Left: A German flamethrower team attacks a defensive strongpoint. One of the most important German abilities was their successful integration of the efforts of all arms into a combined team.

Right: Although its modest performance and vulnerability to attack had been shown up in the Battle of Britain, the Stuka dive bomber remained an important component in the German armory during the 1941 campaign and beyond.

Below, far left: A German tank closes in on Soviet positions in a burning village. By the winter of 1941 combat and other losses had reduced the German armored divisions to only a handful of tanks each.

Below left: A German 8cm mortar crew in action in the Ukraine. Most armies employed weapons of roughly this caliber with the support companies of their infantry battalions.

Below: German artillery weapons employed in the close range street battles for Zhitomir in the Ukraine.

Right: The I-16 fighter entered Soviet service during the Spanish Civil War and was notable for its good rate of climb, maneuverability and heavy armament. Still in service in 1941, it was by then outclassed by the best foreign designs.

Below: Close range combat in a wintry Soviet village.

Bottom: By directives issued early in 1941 Hitler gave control of any territories captured from the Soviets to the SS. Assassination squads followed the advancing troops with orders to round up such as Jews and Communist Party members and murder them. Hundreds of thousands of killings resulted.

By early February 1941 the British forces had won a remarkable series of victories against their Italian opponents. Since the start of the British offensive less than two months previously a force never stronger than 2 divisions had destroyed 10 Italian divisions and taken 130,000 prisoners for the loss of less than 2000 dead and wounded. Hitler could not allow his Italian ally to be so easily defeated so on 12 February an up-and-coming young German General, Erwin Rommel arrived in Tripoli, two days before the first of his force, soon to be known as the Afrika Korps.

Right: A German Mk III tank in typical African desert terrain.

Below: The British Middle East command in 1941 included far more than just the operations in North Africa, being responsible for Palestine, where this mounted unit is seen training in 1940; East Africa, where a difficult campaign was being fought against the Italians; Iraq, where a pro-German rising was put down in May; and Syria, where the Vichy French authorities were replaced after fighting during the summer.

Above: German tanks and supplies are unloaded at a North African port. The fighting in North Africa was remarkable for its dramatic swings of fortune which were caused in large part by how effectively the Germans could transport (and the Allies interrupt) supplies to their forces in the theater.

Above right: A German reconnaissance team encounters difficult sandy conditions.

Below: The crew of a German self-propelled anti-tank gun hunts for targets on a chilly desert morning. Their equipment is a Czech-made 4.7cm gun mounted on an old Panzer I chassis, a powerful combination in these earlier years of the war.

Far left: General Sir Claude Auchinleck took over as the British Commander in Chief, Middle East in July 1941.

Left: Admiral Andrew Cunningham commanded the British Mediterranean Fleet from the beginning of the war until April 1942.

Below: The Italian commander in East Africa, the Duke of Aosta, inspects a guard of honor after his surrender to the British in May 1941.

Above right: A Fieseler Storch light reconnaissance aircraft comes in to land at a desert strip.

Above, far right: A Panzer III leads an armored column. This vehicle is armed with the 3.7cm gun with which the Mk III began the war.

Below: British Matilda tanks ready to move off into the desert. These had been effective weapons against the Italians in 1940-41 but did less well against the more sophisticated German tactics.

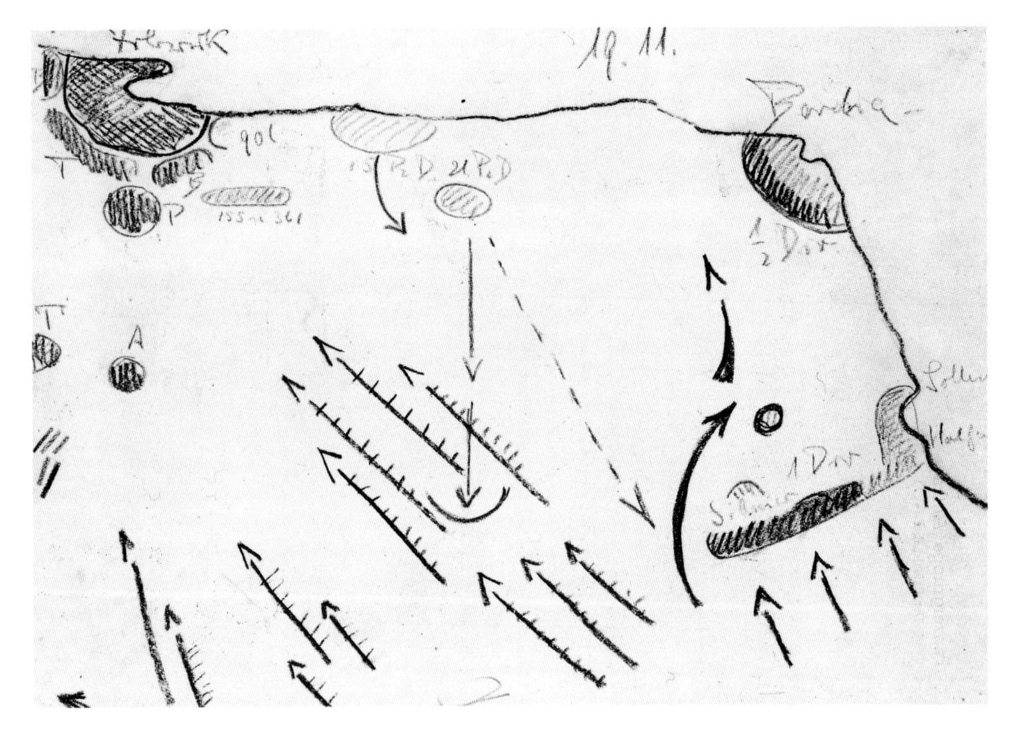

Left: General Rommel's own sketch map of his plans for operations on 19 November 1941. The British attacks can be seen coming from the bottom right of the sketch and the counter moves of Rommel's two Panzer Divisions, 15th and 21st, are also shown.

Below left: Rommel in conversation with an Italian commander. In North Africa Rommel was in the difficult position of being responsible to his own high command and to the Italians who supplied the majority of the Axis force but whom he did not really trust.

Below: The British battleship HMS *Nelson* is clearly down by the bows after being hit by an Italian torpedo plane while escorting a supply convoy from Gibraltar to the island of Malta. The British had believed at the start of the war that Malta was indefensible but in the event mounted numerous massive supply operations in an attempt to keep the island safe and to enable Malta-based forces to strike at the Axis supply lines to Africa. Many commentators believe that the Germans and Italians would have done better to have tried to land on the island, probably during 1942 after Rommel had won his second major victory in the desert.

Above left: America moves closer to war. President Roosevelt, wearing a mourning armband in memory of his recently deceased mother, broadcasts to the American people on 11 September 1941. He announced on that day that he had given US warships orders to 'shoot on sight' against German ships or U-Boats in the western Atlantic which he described as American defensive waters. This followed an incident on 4 September when the USS *Greer* and a German U-Boat were in action.

Left: Colonel Dwight D. Eisenhower (left), Chief of Staff of IX Army Corps, in conversation with one of his officers during maneuvers in June 1941. It was typical of the expansion of the US forces then under way that within two years of this Eisenhower would be a four-star general and the Allied Commander-in-Chief in the Mediterranean.

Below: The pilots of 133 Squadron, the second of three American volunteer squadrons within the RAF formed in 1940-41, before America's entry to the war.

Left: Burning fuel oil flames across Pearl Harbor.

Below left: The battleship *Arizona* burns from the Japanese attacks.

Right: The destroyers *Cassin* and *Downes* lie wrecked in the foreground and behind them is the comparatively lightly hit battleship *Pennsylvania*.

Below: The architect of the Pearl Harbor attack, Admiral Yamamoto.

Far left: Left to right, General Wavell, Commander-in-Chief of the newly-created (January 1942) ABDA (Australian-British-Dutch-American) command in the East Indies, Admiral Hart of the US Asiatic Fleet, and General Brett, commanding US troops in Australia.

Left: Vice Admiral Tom Phillips (right) and his chief of staff, Rear Admiral Paliser, at Singapore shortly before the outbreak of the Japanese war. Phillips commanded the battleship *Prince of Wales* and the battlecruiser *Repulse*.

Below: The *Prince of Wales* shortly after arriving in Singapore.

Right: Japanese troops bring light artillery into action to support their rapid advance.

Below left: Lieutenant General Percival commanded the British land forces in Malaya.

Left: Japanese civilians are rounded up in Manila for internment at the outbreak of war. In fact the Japanese advance in the early stages of the war benefited greatly by information previously collected by Japanese 'visitors' to the areas now attacked.

Right: Field Marshal Sugiyama, Chief of Staff of the Japanese Army at the time of the outbreak of war.

Far right: Large parts of the force defending the Philippines were locally recruited such as these Filipino 'Scouts'. The equipment and training of the Filipino forces were very poor, however.

Below right: Men of a US Marine unit await their orders during the defense of Luzon.

Below: Japanese troops land in Lingayen Gulf, Luzon, on 22 December 1941, as their attack on the Philippines began in earnest.

1942

The year of 1942 saw a series of battles that can rightly be described as turning points in the war – Midway, Stalingrad, and, in a smaller way, El Alamein. As the year began, however, all this lay very much in the future.

The first four months of the year saw a virtually unbroken sequence of successes for the Japanese in which they conquered Malaya, the Philippines, Burma and the Dutch East Indies. In May they received their first check in the naval battle of the Coral Sea, the first naval engagement in history fought entirely by aircraft and in which the opposing fleets never came into direct contact. Although this battle disrupted one Japanese offensive (to seize Papua-New Guinea) the Japanese had become infected with 'victory disease' as a later commentaor described it, and planned a major new attack in another area also. The result was the Battle of Midway in which, in a matter of hours, the core of the Japanese fleet, four aircraft carriers, were sent to the bottom with many of their pilots.

The crucial battles of the Pacific war for the remainder of 1942 were the land, sea and air engagements around Guadalcanal in the Solomon Islands. Although these were very hard fought and by no means always to America's advantage, by the end of the year it was clear that Japan had passed its peak and America could only grow stronger.

The winter months at the beginning of 1942 saw the Soviets, like the Japanese, continue their successful offensive of late 1941. Gradually the Germans recovered their organisation and halted the attacks as spring approached. With the arrival of summer, new German attacks could begin. Although the German forces were still far more skilled than their opponents, it is worth noting that, following the manpower losses they had already sustained, they were sufficiently weakened as not to be able to attack all along the front as they had in 1941. Hitler instead would insist on two main objectives, Stalingrad and the oilfields of the Caucasus region, but even this division of effort would be too much. Again the Soviets prepared a winter counter-offensive at the end of the year. The German armies at Stalingrad were cut off, German counterattacks were held, and soon all the German armies in southern Russia were in rapid retreat.

Fluctuating fortunes had also been the theme of battles in the Mediterranean and North Africa. Led by Rommel's Afrika Korps, in January and February the Axis forces recovered almost all the ground lost to the British attacks of 1941 while in June they took Tobruk and in July pushed on into Egypt. General Montgomery took over the British Eighth Army defending Egypt and in October and November his victory at El Alamein began a definitive German retreat. A few days later Operation Torch, the Anglo-US landing in north-west Africa, began and by the end of the year these troops and the Eighth Army from the east had recaptured much of the north African coast.

Other issues occupying the attention of the Allied military commanders in 1942 were the progress of the U-Boat war and the expansion of bomber attacks on Germany (so far still being conducted by the British alone). The year should also be notorious for decisions taken far from the fighting fronts in Germany. Persecution of the Jews had always been a part of Nazi policy and before 1942 many thousands had indeed been murdered or ill-treated in other hideous ways whether in the slave-labor camps of the Reich, or in the Polish ghettos, or by the SS extermination squads which had followed the German armies into Russia. On 20 January 1942 a meeting of top Nazis (the so-called Wannsee conference) agreed on a new scale of evil – the 'final solution' to the 'Jewish problem' was to be the complete and systematic extermination of all of Europe's Jews. A group of camps whose sole mission was to kill were established (Auschwitz-Birkenau was the most notorious) and mass transportation to their gas chambers began. The Nazis probably murdered between 5.5 and 6 million Jews and with them large numbers of such other 'subhuman' groups (as the Nazis termed them) as gypsies, homosexuals, and the mentally and physically handicapped. This was the worst of the Nazis' many crimes.

Left: Newly appointed to command Eighth Army in North Africa, General Montgomery watches training maneuvers from the turret of a Grant tank.

Above right: Crewmen are rescued by a destroyer from the sinking carrier *Hornet* at the Battle of Santa Cruz on 26 October.

Right: An Australian-crewed 6-pounder antitank gun at full recoil during fighting in the desert in July. Many of the Australian units in North Africa were withdrawn home to face the Japanese. This weakening of the Allied force in Africa was one of the causes of the German success in that theater in the early months of 1942.

Previous page: A destroyer rescues crew from the *Yorktown* at Midway.

Above: The Japanese Mitsubishi Zero fighter was a great shock to the Allied air forces when they first encountered it at the opening of the Pacific War. Japanese pilots were believed to be poor and their aircraft worse, while instead the Zero was the most maneuverable and potent aircraft in the sky. This example is shown after capture and under evaluation by American technicians later in the war.

Above right: Japanese tanks continue their rapid advance during the conquest of Burma. The Japanese deployed few tanks in their capture of Malaya and Burma and these were poorly designed by European standards. They were effective in these campaigns, however, because their enemies' antitank equipment was even scantier.

Left: The Stars and Stripes is lowered on Corregidor Island in Manila Bay after this last strongpoint fell to the Japanese on 6 May 1942.

Right: Japanese troops rush into Rangoon, 7 March 1942.

Above: British and Australian prisoners of war at Changi, Singapore, shortly after their capture.

Left: General MacArthur (left) and General Sutherland, his chief of staff, on Corregidor Island, shortly before MacArthur was ordered to escape to Australia.

Top right: One of the first setbacks the Japanese received was in fighting at Milne Bay in Eastern New Guinea where this Australian is shown with a knocked-out Japanese tank.

Center right: Before America went to war a group of volunteer American pilots was already assisting the Chinese Nationalists against the Japanese. These 'Flying Tigers', were led by Colonel (later General) Claire Chennault (left).

Right: Japanese troops land on Hong Kong island.

Left: Japanese treatment of their prisoners was often a confusing mixture of occasional kindness and decency with the more common harshness and cruelty. This prisoner is clearly receiving appropriate medical treatment.

Below left: An improvised bridge helps these Japanese troops continue their advance in Burma.

Right: Wounded American soldiers go back for treatment during the New Guinea campaign.

Below right: After America entered the war, the Shark's Mouth insignia previously used by the American Volunteer Group, the Flying Tigers, was widely used by the USAAF aircraft operating over China. Here a group of P-40 pilots run to their aircraft. The P-40 had also commonly been used by the Flying Tigers.

24

On 18 April 1942 American B-25 Mitchell bombers commanded by Lieutenant Colonel Jimmie Doolittle successfully bombed the Japanese capital, Tokyo, and other targets and then flew on to China. President Roosevelt announced that the aircraft had come from 'Shangri-La' and morale in the US was accordingly boosted. Very little material damage was done but the moral effect in Japan was very great. The Japanese government were shocked that the Emperor might have come to harm in the attack and the attack contributed to the decision shortly to be taken that Japan would attempt to expand the perimeter already captured. This would lead to the fateful battles of Midway and the Coral Sea. In fact, in an unprecedented feat for such large aircraft, the bombers had taken off from the carrier *Hornet*. Several members of the aircrews were captured by the Japanese after their landings in China and later executed.

Far left: Doolittle (front left) with Admiral Mitscher who led the *Hornet* task force and, behind, some of Doolittle's men.

Left: Ready to take off.

Below: On the way to Tokyo.

Left: Admiral of the Fleet Sir Dudley Pound was Britain's First Sea Lord (Chief of Naval Staff) 1939-43. For much of that time he was also Chairman of Britain's Chiefs of Staff Committee.

Below: HMS *Lookout* was the only one of eight British 'L' class destroyers to survive the war. This type carried a main armament of six 4.7-inch guns.

Right: Admiral Pound seen with his American counterpart, Admiral Ernie King. King led his service with great vigor throughout the war though he has since been criticised for devoting more US naval resources to the Pacific campaign in the years 1942-44 than his political masters intended.

Above: It was very quickly obvious that the presence of air cover with a merchant ship convoy not only helped secure the ships from air attack but from submarine threat also. Full-size aircraft carriers, later to be known as fleet carriers, were always likely to be too scarce and precious to be used in this work so various expedients to get aircraft to sea in some other way were tried. The most successful of these was the building of the smaller escort carrier type. The first ever escort carrier was HMS *Audacity*, shown here, a converted captured German banana boat, which entered service with the Atlantic convoys in June 1941 and was sunk on a Gibraltar convoy in December the same year.

Above: Admiral Raeder led Hitler's fleet from long before the war until 1943. Although war experience would show that Germany's best naval weapon was the submarine, Raeder had favored a battleship-building program in the traditional manner.

Above left: The crew of a U-Boat line up for inspection before setting out on an Atlantic patrol. The picture shows the crew of *U.203*, a Type VIIC boat in the French port of Brest in 1942.

Left: As well as their main operations on the North Atlantic convoy routes, the U-Boats also served in more distant waters. The spiral devices seen on the lowered periscopes were designed to reduce tell-tale spray when the periscopes were in use.

Above right: Signallers at work on a Royal Navy ship.

Right: A successful U-Boat returns to base after the US joined the war. The banners on the periscope show the tonnage of the ships believed to be sunk and the flag is stated to be from the SS *Stella Lykes*. The U-Boat is *U.582*.

Above: US troops arrive in Iceland to relieve the garrison.

Right: In the 'destroyers for bases' deal of September 1940 Britain had been given 50 old US destroyers in return for leases on various bases in the Western Hemisphere being granted to the US. The destroyers were a welcome reinforcement to the British escort forces in the Atlantic battle but needed much work and modification before they were fully efficient. This is HMS *Clare*, shown with two of her funnels removed, the visible evidence of the replacement of two of her boilers by long range fuel tanks. Endurance was more valuable in an escort than high speed.

Right: Like Hitler, Mussolini enjoyed the creation of public monuments in a grand style. This is the edifice known to the British as 'Marble Arch', after the broadly similar construction in London, a landmark on the road to Tripoli, seen here with various Eighth Army trucks in 1942.

Below: One of the most notable German air aces of the North African fighting, and indeed of the war as a whole, was Joachim Marseille, seen here as a Leutnant with 3/JG.27 in March 1942. His aircraft is a Bf 109F/4 Trop.

T33417

Far left: A German tank column passes an abandoned British Bren gun carrier during the desert fighting.

Left: The escort carrier USS *Santee* off the African coast during Operation Torch in November 1942.

Right: German infantrymen wait in their foxhole for the time to attack.

Below: An Italian bomber burns on an airfield briefly captured by the British as their advance petered out at the start of 1942.

Above: New Zealand infantry with their Vickers machine gun in a defensive position near El Alamein in July 1942 as Rommel's final great offensive was being halted.

Above left: The capture of Tobruk earlier in the campaign was a great and unexpected setback for the Allied forces. Rommel here is consulting with the Italian General Azzi just after the port fell in June 1942.

Above: One of the consequences of the fall of Tobruk was the American decision to send some of the latest Sherman tanks to the British Eighth Army. Deception was also a feature of the desert campaign and this recently-arrived Sherman is shrouded in a canvas cover to give it the appearance, from the air, of a truck.

Below: Infantry of the Afrika Korps in typically featureless desert terrain.

Left: A British soldier waits beside his Bren gun, mounted for anti-aircraft defense, in a North African town.

Right: Is it a truck? Is it a tank? Part of the considerable deception effort undertaken by the Allies before the Battle of El Alamein.

Below right: A weary-looking Rommel gives instructions to one of his officers. By the late summer of 1942 Rommel was clearly worn out and sick. He had actually returned to Germany for medical treatment when the Allied attack at El Alamein began, a token of how well the Allies had concealed their plans.

Below: A British mortar battery, equipped with the heavy, 4.2-inch mortar, comes under enemy artillery fire.

Left: The principal British heavy artillery weapon for most of the war was the 5.5-inch gun, shown in this carefully-posed picture in a desert setting.

Right: Sherman tanks during training for the El Alamein battle. Note how the wartime censor has scratched out the unit markings from their various positions on the front of the tanks.

Below: A German Sd Kfz 233 heavy armored car armed with a short 7.5cm gun dwarfs its ally, an Italian Semovente light self-propelled gun, Tunisia, late 1942.

Left: The weapon most feared by the Allied tank crews throughout the war was the 'eighty-eight', the famed 8.8cm antitank and antiaircraft gun.

Bottom left: One of the gimmicks which General Montgomery employed to aid morale was his custom of wearing a hat decorated with a selection of the cap badges of the units under his command.

Right: The first stages of the advance after the final breakthrough at El Alamein were hampered by heavy rain.

Below: A column of Shermans is led by their command tank during the advance.

Left: Colonel David Stirling, founder of the SAS (Special Air Service) Regiment with a patrol from the unit.

Right: General Montgomery gives tactical directions to a group of Eighth Army officers.

Far right: The battleship USS *Massachusetts* supported the US forces landing at Casablanca on 8 November 1942 as part of Operation Torch. The *Massachusetts* fought a gunnery duel with the French *Jean Bart*, armed but immobile at the port.

Below: American forces come ashore during the Torch operation. In order to appease French opinion, still hostile to the British since the events of 1940, the Torch operation was presented at the time as principally an American undertaking.

Above right: Advancing from east and west, soldiers of the British Eighth and First Armies meet in Tunisia shortly before the German surrender in 1943.

Right: Sailors remove cork insulation from a bulkhead aboard the cruiser USS *Augusta* as a fire precaution before she goes into action at the start of the Torch landings.

Below: US troops march inland from their landing beaches. Resistance to the landings was generally light and the local Vichy French forces were fairly quickly won over to the Allied cause.

Left: Secondary armament of the heavy cruiser USS *Northampton* in action during an early Pacific war engagement.

Below: Antiaircraft machine gunners aboard an American carrier anxiously scan the skies looking for another Japanese attack.

Left: Aircraft on the deck of the carrier *Enterprise* early in 1942. The red circle in the center of the aircraft's star insignia was deleted not long after because, in the heat of combat, it could be mistaken for the Japanese symbol.

Right: The principal American success during the Battle of the Coral Sea was the sinking of the Japanese light fleet carrier *Shoho*. An American torpedo aircraft is shown here turning away after dropping its load, aimed to hit the already damaged Japanese vessel.

Below right & bottom: Two views of the doomed American carrier *Lexington* at the Battle of the Coral Sea. Although ostensibly this was a far more valuable loss than the Japanese *Shoho*, the two larger Japanese carriers present, *Zuikaku* and *Shokaku*, both lost heavily from their air groups and would not be available to take part in the subsequent Battle of Midway unlike the other American carrier, the *Enterprise* which was patched up in time.

Left: One of the Japanese casualties in the Midway engagement was the heavy cruiser *Mogami* seen here crippled by the American attacks.

Below left: The ill-fated USS *Yorktown* is photographed by one of her own aircraft shortly before Midway.

Right: Admiral Nagumo was in direct tactical command of the Japanese carriers at Midway but was placed at a substantial disadvantage by the wasteful dispersal of the Japanese forces caused by their over-complicated plan and by the excellent intelligence information of the Americans, based on the work of their code-breaking service.

Below: Damage control parties at work on the flight deck of the *Yorktown*, Midway, 4 June 1942.

Four views of the carrier *Yorktown* under attack and damaged at Midway. In fact the *Yorktown* did not sink until the 7th when attacked by a Japanese submarine.

Left: The damaged smokestack and superstructure of the *Yorktown* after the second Japanese bomb hit. This hit extinguished the fires in five of the carrier's six boilers.

Right: Aircraft losses were heavy on both sides at Midway. This Avenger bomber which landed back on Midway Island badly damaged was the sole survivor of its squadron.

Below: Out of fuel, a Dauntless ditches beside an American heavy cruiser.

Above: German Junkers transport aircraft at an airfield near Smolensk in March 1942. The Luftwaffe was able successfully to supply some isolated units cut off by the Soviet advance in this winter campaign, a precedent which was to have dire consequences when Stalingrad was surrounded later in the year.

Above left: A German self-propelled gun passes by an infantry position in the high summer of 1942.

Left: With the heavy losses of the winter campaign of 1941-42, an increasing proportion of the Axis force on the Eastern Front came to be non-German in 1942. The troops shown here are Rumanians and it was to be Rumanian armies that were the first targets of the Russian counteroffensive at Stalingrad.

Right: For the moment, however, the German advance continued to make great territorial gains, but unlike in the last summer campaign, comparatively few prisoners were taken.

Left: By the summer of 1942 the factories transported east from the western parts of the USSR and re-established in Siberia were beginning to get into proper production. This factory characteristically is producing sub-machine guns. Compared with other armies, the Soviet forces used a higher proportion of these weapons and fewer rifles in infantry units.

Below left: The soldiers taking the compulsory oath of loyalty to Hitler are not German but Caucasian volunteers enlisting with the German forces. If it had not been for the needless brutality and atrocities of the German occupation of the western USSR, it is certainly possible that substantial forces could have been raised to join the Germans from among the many who had good reason to hate Stalin's rule. A senior Soviet general, General Vlasov, did defect to the Germans after being captured in 1942 but was only allowed to found his so-called Russian Liberation Army late in 1944 by which time it was obviously too late to have any important effect.

Right: German railroad troops cheerfully proclaim Stalingrad as their destination, August 1942.

Below: Winter, and a different story, as Soviet infantry advance.

Top & left: Although the German advance into the Caucasus, at the same time as the Stalingrad offensive, was designed to capture oilfields, these photos of the time show operations towards the mountains of the region. German propaganda made much of the fact that their troops reached Mount Elbrus, the highest in the area.

Above: Heavily forested regions were also the scene of many Eastern Front battles.

Right: Russian winters may be cold but, especially in the south summers can be extremely hot. This German machine gunner is equipped with a camouflage net which would also serve to protect against flies.

Opposite page, top left: German troops on the Finnish sector of the front improvise a temporary anti-aircraft mounting for their MG34.

Opposite page, top right: Undoubtedly the most famous Soviet general of the war, Georgi Zhukov. Zhukov first came to prominence in border battles against the Japanese in 1939 and later played a leading role in every major campaign against the Germans from the Battle for Moscow in 1941 on.

Top: Soviet infantry on the attack, supposedly at Stalingrad, but actually a scene from a propaganda film.

Above: A German soldier abandons his blazing tank.

Left: Soviet troops overrun a German airfield.

The first significant US counter move against the Japanese began what was to be the long and bitterly contested Battle for Guadalcanal.

Above left: The first steps were US landings on Guadalcanal itself and the nearby and much smaller islands of Tulagi and Gavatu (shown here). Tulagi and Gavutu were quickly captured.

Below: Japanese 'Betty' bombers attack the transports off Guadalcanal on August 8th.

Above left: An anti-aircraft gun crew aboard the carrier *Wasp* enjoy a hasty snack on 7 August 1942, the first day of the Guadalcanal landings. The supporting naval forces for the landings were quickly withdrawn by their cautious commander, Admiral Fletcher, before the Marines' supplies were fully ashore, a decision which probably substantially and unnecessarily delayed the campaign.

Above: A bomb explodes aboard the carrier *Enterprise* during the Battle of the Eastern Solomons, 24 August 1942.

Above & below: Two views of the sinking of the carrier *Wasp* on 15 September 1942 while she was engaged in covering supply shipments to Guadalcanal. The *Wasp* fell victim to the Japanese submarine *I.19* which also damaged the battleship *North Carolina* and sank a destroyer on the same day.

Left: US transports off Guadalcanal, a picture certainly taken at the very start of the campaign since it was taken from the heavy cruiser *Chicago*, which was badly damaged early in the morning of August 9th.

Above & above left: Two views of the USS *Hornet* taking heavy punishment before sinking during the Battle of Santa Cruz, 26 October 1942. *Above*, a damaged Japanese aircraft is about to crash on board and, *left*, a torpedo splashes down and is seemingly certain to hit.

Left: Despite their considerable successes in the naval battles of the campaign, on land the Japanese lost heavily throughout the Guadalcanal battles.

Right: General Hyakutake commanded the Japanese 17th Army based at Rabaul and in particular was responsible for the all-out Japanese effort to retake Guadalcanal in October.

Left: Major General Vandegrift commanded the Marines on Guadalcanal throughout the first difficult months.

Right: A photograph, taken from a dead Japanese on Guadalcanal, of a machine gun crew from the Japanese naval landing forces.

Below right: Japanese corpses lie huddled together in graphic evidence of the failure of yet another mass infantry attack. The virtually suicidal bravery of the Japanese soldiers was no substitute for tactical sophistication or better firepower.

Below: Japanese transport ships lie beached and burning on Guadalcanal following the decisive defeat of their naval forces in the Naval Battle of Guadalcanal 13-15 November 1942.

Left: US Army Chief of Staff General George C. Marshall confers with his political superior, Secretary of War Henry L. Stimson. Although Stimson was a Republican, Roosevelt brought him in to his cabinet in June 1940, even before Roosevelt was re-elected for his third term. Stimson strongly opposed American isolationism.

Below left: The actress Marlene Dietrich in Cleveland, Ohio, on a tour to promote the sale of War Bonds in July 1942.

Right & below: Two views of the terrible conditions in the Warsaw ghetto. In German-occupied Poland the country's Jews were confined in tiny districts in the cities soon after the Germans moved in. Rations were minimal and hard labor was demanded. Many thousands died and this was even before the extermination of the Jews became formal Nazi policy as it did in the early part of 1942.

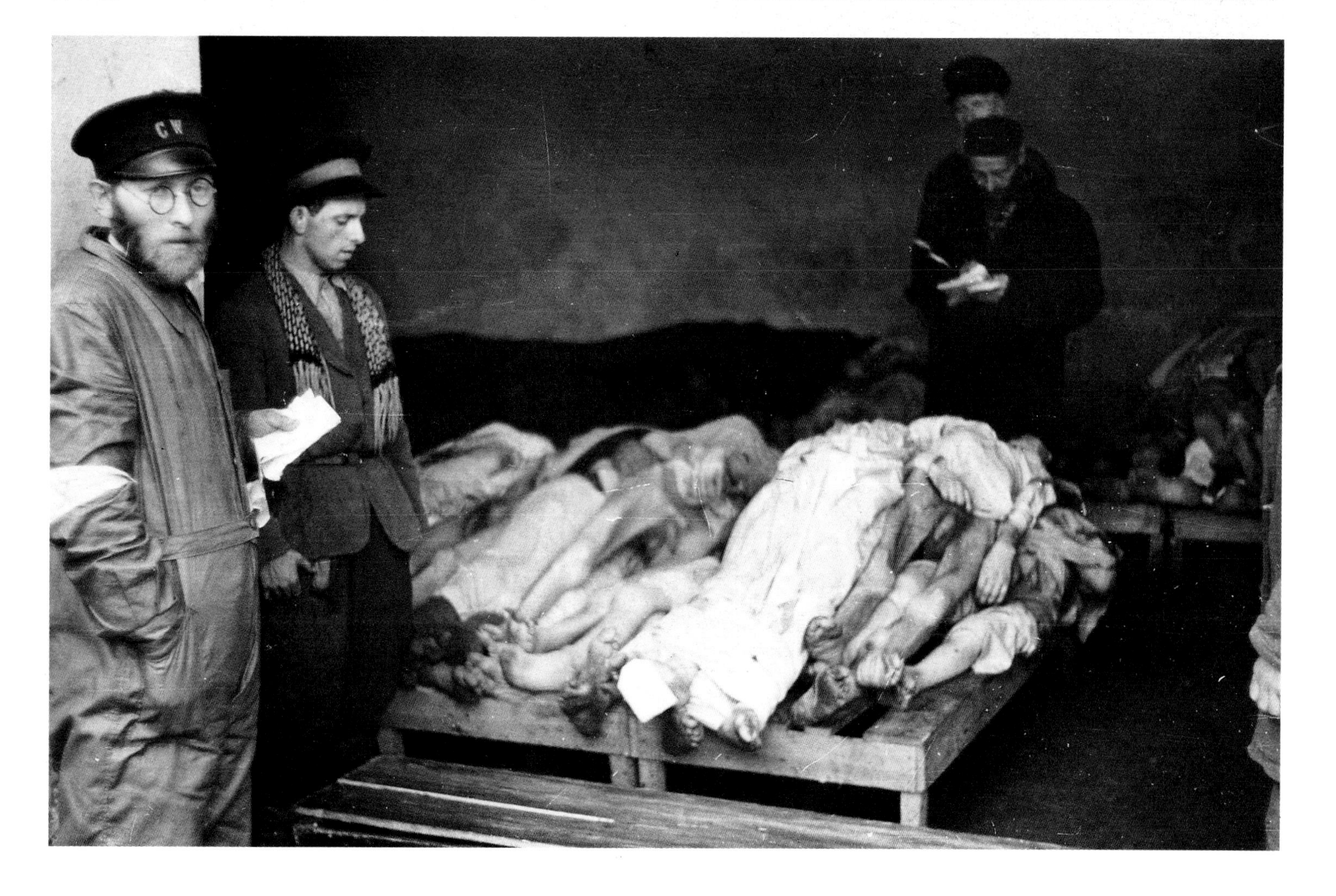

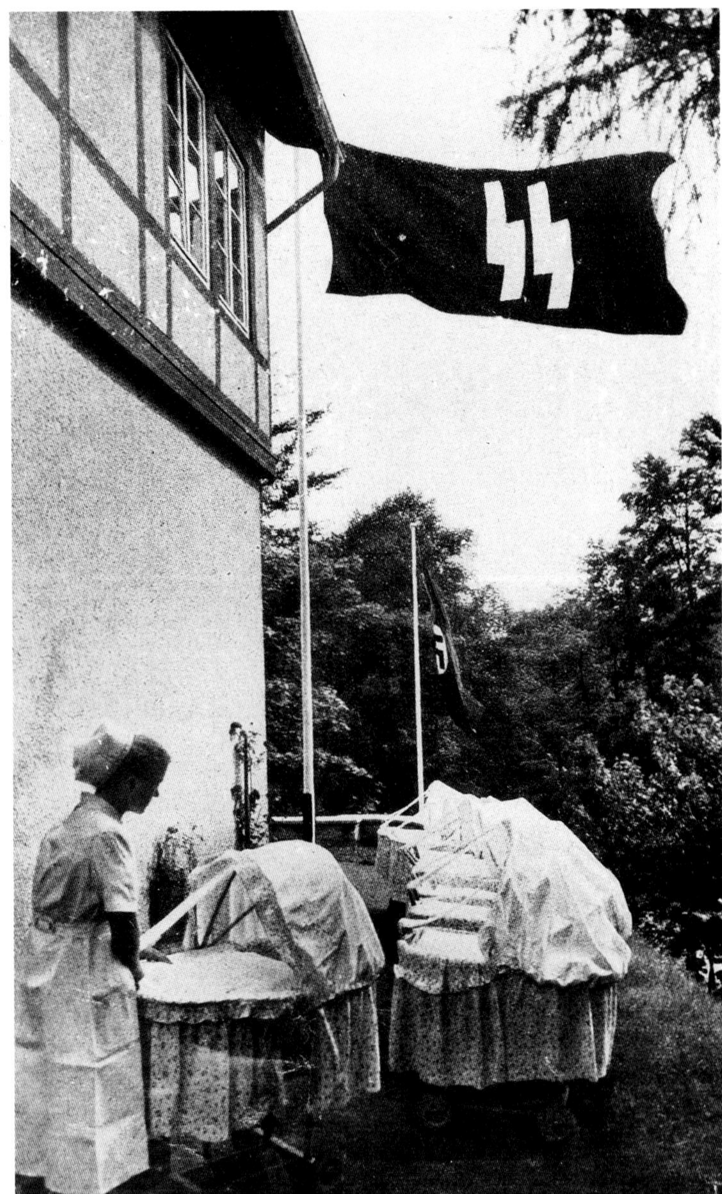

Top, far left: Obergruppenführer Reinhard Heydrich, one of the most evil of the Nazi leaders. He died, following an attack by Czech resistance fighters, in June 1942. The Germans conducted a program of savage reprisals including the murder of the entire adult population of the village of Lidice.

Above left: One of the more bizarre results of Nazi racial policies was the establishment of SS nurseries to care for the illegitimate offspring of the supposedly racially pure and superior SS men. In another strange touch many of the children of Lidice were taken to Germany and are thought to have had identities changed and been adopted by German families.

Above: The main interest in this photo is not the house but the small structure nearer the camera and to the left. This radar installation at Bruneval in northern France was the target of a British commando raid in February 1942 to seize radar equipment for evaluation.

Other examples of German radar equipment are (*left*) a'Freya' apparatus at Brest in France and (*right*) a 'Wurzburg' similar to the Bruneval equipment. The technical battle to unravel the enemy's secrets was an important side issue in the air war and in particular in the struggle between night bombers and fighters.

1943

1943 was the year in which both the Germans and the Japanese began to yield up significant areas of captured territory to the Allies.

The last German forces at Stalingrad surrendered at the beginning of February but by then the Germans had avoided the still greater disasters which had seemed to threaten the whole of their forces in the southern USSR at the tail end of 1942. Under the talented leadership of General von Manstein the Germans were even able to win a significant success in counterattacks in the Kharkov region by mid March. Heartened by this the Germans again planned a summer offensive, this time around Kursk. When they attacked in July they were defeated in the largest tank battle of the war and a remorseless Soviet advance began instead.

At the same time as the Battle of Kursk, British and American forces began landing in Sicily, having completed the capture of North Africa by early May. In little more than a month Sicily had been taken and Mussolini's government had been deposed by the Italians themselves. At the start of September Allied forces landed on the Italian mainland and the new Italian government surrendered. The Germans fought on in Italy, only gradually being pushed back to the north by the Allied advance.

The early months of 1943 saw the climax of the Battle of the Atlantic. In March the U-Boats sank 72 ships from north Atlantic convoys and came close to crippling the convoy system. By May there had been a transformation. Forty-one U-Boats were sunk that month and Admiral Doenitz ordered an end to operations on the main convoy routes. Thereafter, although they were a constant threat, losses inflicted by the U-Boats were comparatively minor for the rest of the war.

British bombers had been attacking Germany in growing strength since 1940 and in 1943 they were joined by American Flying Fortresses and Liberators. The British operated at night but the Americans believed in daytime precision attacks. In the absence of long-range fighter escorts this policy was proved to be misguided by the losses in the great raids on the German ball-bearing factories at Schweinfurt in August and October. In December, however, the desired long-range escort, the P-51B Mustang, entered service and a transformation of the whole air war was set in train.

Allied gains were less spectacular in 1943 in the war against Japan. In Burma on the Asian mainland nothing in fact was gained. The modest offensive in the Arakan region (begun in 1942), which was all that British resources would allow, was heavily defeated and repulsed in March-May. Allied morale in Burma was improved to some extent by an expedition behind Japanese lines by a special force, the Chindits, but their concrete achievements were minimal. Another hopeful pointer for the future was the appointment, after the debacle in the Arakan, of General Slim to lead the British and Indian troops in Burma. The events of 1944 would prove him a most able commander.

In the southern Pacific, throughout the year, the Americans and Australians extended their hold on eastern New Guinea and, after the completion of the Guadalcanal campaign, also began to advance up the Solomons chain. In November a major new offensive began – the drive across the central Pacific by the US Navy's aircraft carriers and amphibious forces. The first targets, Tarawa and Makin in the Gilbert Islands, were very fiercely defended but were captured nonetheless. Here, as elsewhere, further Allied advances were clearly being prepared for 1944.

Above: The bearded Brigadier Wingate, the unconventional leader of the Chindits, with a group of his men.

Left: Marines rehearsing landing operations from the transport *McCawley*. 1943 was the year in which the US began truly to develop its amphibious forces.

Right: Generals Eisenhower and Clark at a conference to plan developments on the Italian front, October 1943. Behind them, with pipe, is General Lucas who would lead the Anzio landings in January 1944.

Previous page: US Marine Mitchell bombers during a raid on the Japanese base at Rabaul.

Above: The light cruiser USS *Boise* carries out a night bombardment of Japanese positions on the north coast of New Guinea in February 1943.

Above left: A formation of B-25 Mitchell medium bombers passes over an Allied convoy. The bombers are on their way to attack Rabaul, for long the main Japanese base in the area, but eventually to be isolated, bypassed and 'left to wither on the vine'.

Left: One Japanese fighter struggles into the air (right) while a delayed action bomb drops by parachute in the foreground and other bombs explode in the background.

Right: Australian troops move up to the front at Sananada, scene of fierce battles in the early days of 1943.

Above: Landings at Nassau Bay on New Guinea began in July 1943. Here troops are loaded into landing craft from PT boats.

Right: Generals MacArthur (left) and Kenney at their headquarters in Australia. MacArthur commanded the Southwest Pacific Area and Kenney was his air force chief.

Right: Russian civilians mourn victims left behind by the retreating Germans in one of the most famous images of the dreadful struggle on the Eastern Front.

Below: A Soviet soldier hangs out the Red Flag and contemplates what is left of the recaptured city of Stalingrad.

Left: Marshal Konstantin Rokossovsky was one of the Soviet Army's leading commanders during the whole of World War II. He is seen here during the Soviet counteroffensive to retake Stalingrad where his forces opened the advance.

Below: Soviet infantry on the attack.

Right: A German StuG III assault gun passes two abandoned Soviet T-34s as a German column moves up in preparation for the Kursk offensive.

Left: Lend Lease in action. A Soviet gun crew leaps down from their US-built White Scout Car. Although the Soviets relied mainly on their own designs of armored vehicles, in trucks and many other areas US supplies were very important.

Right: Perhaps the most famous Soviet aircraft of the war, the Ilyushin 2 'Shturmovik' ground attack aircraft.

Below: Tanks and men of the 3rd SS Panzer Division 'Totenkopf' move up to the front at Kursk. They are obviously not expecting immediate action or the infantry would not be riding in their exposed positions on the tanks.

Below right: A Soviet antitank gun crew in training.

Far left: Partisan operations behind the German lines were extensively developed by the Soviets, although this image seems rather posed.

Left: General von Manstein studies a map with a group of his officers. Manstein is often described as the most able German general of the war. His victory at Kharkov in the spring of 1943 finally halted the long period of Soviet successes from the start of their attacks at Stalingrad.

Right: Croatian artillerymen of the SS Mountain Division 'Handschar' in action.

Below: Soviet officers contemplate a collection of captured German tanks. The Battle of Kursk was the greatest tank battle of the war and the first victory won by the Soviets during the summer on the Eastern Front.

Above: The Ju 87G version of the Stuka was introduced in 1943 and carried a pair of underwing 37mm cannon for the antitank role. The most famous of pilots of this machine was Hans-Ulrich Rudel who was credited with destroying over 500 Soviet tanks.

Right: General Ivan Konev in discussion with one of the members of his staff.

Left: The Germans made extensive use of the giant Me 323 transport aircraft in their rapid build-up of forces in Tunisia in late 1942 and early 1943 but many were shot down by Allied aircraft later in this campaign.

Below: A US Ranger battalion in the Tunisian hills in January 1943.

Above left: US Rangers practice amphibious operations in Algeria, late 1942.

Left: Men of the 16th Infantry move up to reinforce the front near Kasserine, Tunisia, 26th February 1943. In the previous few days veteran German troops had inflicted a substantial defeat on the inexperienced American forces in this sector.

Top: The light cruiser *Savannah* is undamaged in the foreground but two Liberty ships burn behind, following a German air attack on the harbor at Algiers in June 1943.

Right: A British tank crew at work on the 6-pounder gun of their Crusader tank during the final stages of the fighting in Tunisia.

Left: US artillerymen in action with their 105mm howitzer during the Battle of Kasserine. One artillery unit made a notable forced march to reach the fighting from Oran, 800 miles away.

Right: The crew of a British armored car pose happily for the camera as the fighting in Tunisia comes to an end.

Far right: General George Patton looks out over the front shield of his command scout car during the fighting near Gabes, Tunisia, 15th March 1943.

Below: German and Italian prisoners mount up ready for transportation to their camps during the final stages of the Tunisian battle.

8
23
23

Left: A sunken submarine and other damaged ships in the harbor of Bizerta after its capture by the Allies in May 1943.

Below left: By 1943, as this Panzer IV in Tunisia shows, this type of tank had been upgunned with a longer, and thus higher-velocity, 7.5 cm gun.

Right: A British-crewed Sherman tank overlooks a crowd of German prisoners going 'into the bag' at Tunis.

Below: A very neatly equipped American infantryman rehearses operations in co-operation with armored units in a North African town.

Above: Some of the many thousands of Italian prisoners taken in Libya and Tunisia.

Right: Following the very costly victory at Crete in 1941 German paratroops were never again used in large-scale airborne operations but often, as here in Tunisia, as conventional infantry. One of the many inefficient features of the German military administration was the way that competition between top Nazis for personal power led to duplication of effort. By 1943 Luftwaffe divisions (including the paratroops) were absorbing substantial manpower which would probably have been more effectively deployed by the main army units.

Above: The *King George V* Class battleship HMS *Duke of York* in rough Arctic seas. The convoys to north Russia were an important part of the Royal Navy's efforts. The *Duke of York* sank the German battlecruiser *Scharnhorst* during operations around the convoy JW-55B in December 1943.

Right: Gun crew on duty during an Arctic convoy. Some catch what sleep they can despite the cold and damp.

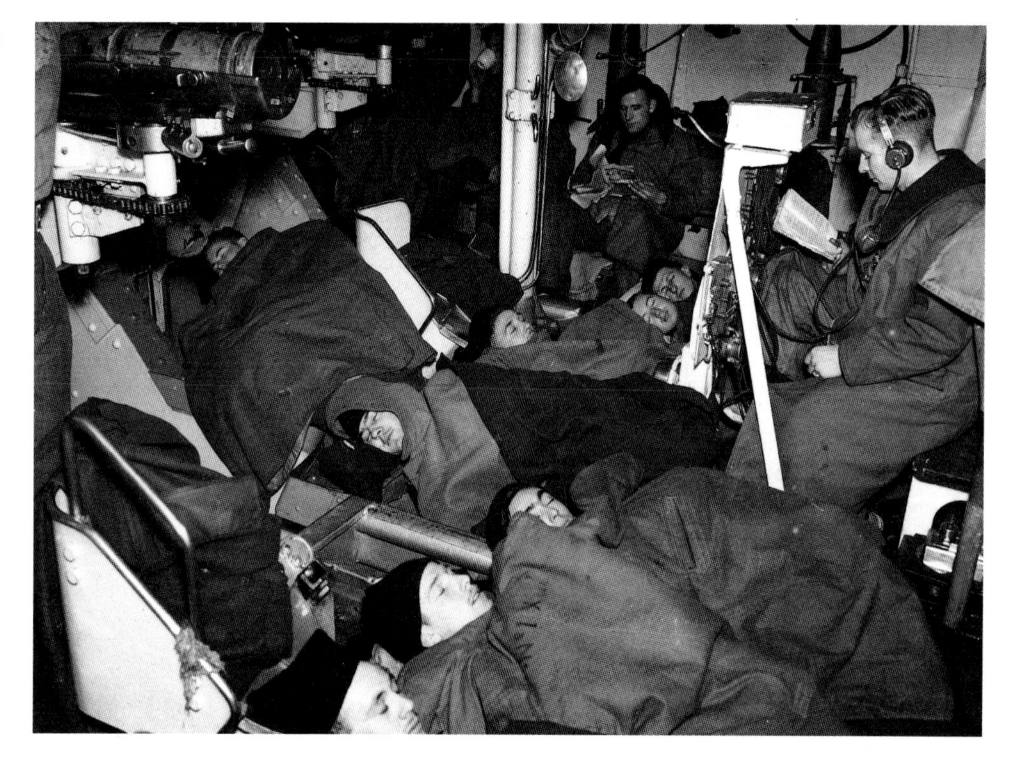

Above: A Consolidated Liberator patrol bomber sets off from England for the Bay of Biscay area. Increased patrols in this area were one contribution to the growing success of the Allied anti-submarine forces that became decisive in May 1943.

Left: Inspection for the crew of a German warship

Right: A U-Boat captain and one of his officers on their return from patrol.

Above: Admiral Doenitz (center) commanded the German submarine force from the start of the war and also became Commander in Chief of the German Navy in January 1943.

Below: A U-Boat leaves its French base for an Atlantic patrol.

K25

Left: At the time this photo was taken the ship shown was HMS *Churchill* but had previously been the USS *Herndon*. Her varied career continued when she was passed to the Soviet Navy in 1944/45 as the *Deiatelnyi*.

Below left: The 'Flower' Class corvette HMS *Azalea*. Nearly 300 ships of this class were built during the war and despite their small size and other disadvantages they played a vital part in the U-Boat war.

Right: US soldiers aboard a transatlantic troop ship. Special precautions were taken to route such vessels away from the possibility of U-Boat attack. The ships used as troop transports were often converted large liners whose high speed also conferred a useful degree of protection.

Bottom right: A U-Boat bunker in the French port of St Nazaire. The British made the mistake of not trying to bomb these bunkers while they were being built. Once they were complete they proved virtually invulnerable to attack until special bombs were introduced late in the war.

Above: B-17 Flying Fortresses during a raid on Occupied Europe.

Below: The crew of the Flying Fortress *Memphis Belle* were the first to complete their allocation of 25 bombing missions.

Above: The very effective raids on Hamburg in late July 1943 were the first in which the radar countermeasure known as 'Window' was used. Window comprised strips of metal foil, shown here being manufactured, which were dropped from aircraft to give false traces on enemy radars.

Left: A British Lancaster bomber during a night attack on Hamburg.

Above left: His Majesty King George VI offers his congratulations to personnel of 617 Squadron after the famous 'Dambusters' raid.

Left: The Republic P-47 Thunderbolt served as a fighter and ground attack aircraft with the US forces. With over 12,500 produced, the P-47D was the most numerous subtype of any fighter in history.

Above: A formation of B-17s is escorted by a P-51 Mustang. The bombers are fitted with the chin turret that early experience over Germany showed to be necessary to defend against fighter attacks from head on.

Right: A group of B-24 Liberator bombers at a US air station. These aircraft had a longer range than their stablemate the Flying Fortress but did not fly as well at high altitude.

L
2107112
VE
L
337675
N
VE

891
864

Above: US medium bombers are prepared for a mission at a wintry airfield 'somewhere in England'.

Above right: Escorting fighters leave condensation trails as they weave above a formation of B-17s. For most of 1943 Allied fighters had insufficient range to escort bombers to targets much inside Germany and the bombers took unacceptable losses as a result.

Left & right: One Flying Fortress that made it home despite heavy damage, and one that very clearly did not.

Above: Men from a US bomber unit pose for the camera in their briefing room at a bomber base in England.

Right: The Focke Wulf 190 first saw service in 1941 when it was for a time superior to any Allied fighter. It was used in various subtypes in every theater where the Germans fought. Over 20,000 of the various versions were built.

Left: The destroyer USS *O'Bannon* shows off her two forward 5-inch guns. This weapon and its related fire control system was probably the best medium caliber armament in service with any navy during the war.

Below: 20mm light anti-aircraft guns on the *O'Bannon*'s quarterdeck. Two more of the five 5-inch mountings fitted on the *Fletcher* Class ships can be seen in the background.

Left: Bodies and debris litter the beach at Tarawa in the Gilbert islands after the short but fierce battle for the tiny island in November 1943. American losses at Tarawa were the worst in history in proportion to the size of the force engaged. Important lessons for future attacks on Japanese-held islands were learned, however.

Below left: US Marines involved in supply loading operations from what had become the base area of Guadalcanal by later in 1943.

Right: Crewmen of the USS *Yorktown* respond to a general quarters alarm during operations in May 1943. This *Yorktown* was the second US aircraft carrier of the same name (the first *Yorktown* was sunk during the Battle of Midway).

Below left: Although by mid 1943 the US naval forces were beginning rapidly to overtake the Japanese, there were still setbacks. Here oily survivors of the sinking of the light cruiser *Helena* are seen aboard the destroyer *Nicholas*, following the Battle of Kula Gulf on 6 July 1943.

Above left: US Navy fighter pilots are briefed by their squadron leader aboard the carrier *Lexington* (the second of the name) during the Gilbert Islands operations in November 1943.

Left: A GI inspects a downed Japanese fighter at Munda on New Georgia.

Above: Flight deck scene aboard the carrier *Monterey* late in 1943. Careful organisation of movements of aircraft, fuel, munitions and crew was essential aboard ship if operations were to be carried out efficiently.

Above right: Construction of an airfield on Bougainville in December 1943. The construction is being carried out by 'Seabees', Navy men who got their name from the phonetic rendering of C.B. for Construction Battalions, their official title. These units played a vital but often unnoticed part in the success of Allied operations.

Right: A Catalina flying boat on patrol over the Aluetian Islands in the North Pacific.

Four views of the US landings on the island of Bougainville and the subsequent fighting there. The landings began on 1 November 1943 at Empress Augusta Bay on the west of the island. This avoided a direct attack on the main Japanese force on the island which was mainly deployed in the south. The American forces quickly established themselves ashore and beat off Japanese attacks. The final important Japanese attacks were in March 1944, although large Japanese forces remained on the island until the end of the war.

Left: The crew of a Marine 75mm pack howitzer stand ready to defend the US positions on Bougainville, December 1943.

Below: A Japanese warship comes under air attack from US bombers.

Above right: The 5-inch guns of a US destroyer blaze into action during a night engagement of the Solomons campaign.

Above, far right: Men of the 2nd Marine Raider Battalion move up to the front on Bougainville with their dogs, used for scouting and running messages.

Below right: Some Marines take a welcome pause in the scanty cover provided by Tarawa's low sea wall.

82A/B-320-F
A-8

Top left: Men of the US 82nd Airborne Division load a Jeep into their Waco glider, ready for the Allied attack on Sicily in July 1943. Many such gliders came down in the sea short of their objectives because of high winds and the inexperience of the crews of the aircraft towing them.

Above left: Generals Mark Clark (left) and George Patton. Clark led US Fifth Army during the mainland battles in Italy while Patton led Seventh Army in Sicily and later Third Army in France and Germany.

Above: Patton with one of his infantry commanders during the fighting on Sicily. Patton was also controversially involved in incidents at this time when he struck and bullied soldiers who were in hospitals suffering from battle fatigue.

Left: Men of the British 51st Highland Division come ashore on Sicily. After the fighting on the island was over this veteran unit was sent back to the UK to help prepare for the invasion of France.

Right: Marshal Pietro Badoglio was the first leader of the Italian government following the deposition of Mussolini in July 1943. Although he initially promised to remain loyal to Germany, in reality he was looking to take Italy out of the war and an armistice with the Allies was concluded in September. The Germans fought on in Italy, nonetheless.

Left: General Patton during the Sicilian campaign.

Right: Men of the British Shropshire Yeomanry Regiment with their 5.5-inch gun on the Italian front in September 1943.

Below: US troops land at Salerno, south of Naples, 9 September 1943, and immediately come under enemy fire. Hitler hoped that by fiercely resisting these early landings, the British and Americans would be discouraged from invading France which they were clearly planning to do.

1-8

Above left: A formal portrait of Mussolini in his days as undisputed Italian leader.

Above, far left: When Mussolini was arrested by the new Italian government which deposed him, Hitler had a rescue operation mounted. A special unit commanded by Otto Skorzeny (seen with Mussolini, *top left*) flew gliders to Mussolini's remote mountain prison (*left*) on 12 September 1943.

Top: Wounded soldiers from the Italian fighting are evacuated to an Allied hospital ship.

Right: Mitchell medium bombers of the 12th Air Force pass over Mount Vesuvius on their way to attack German positions.

Right: Mark Clark was one of the more controversial American leaders of the war. His critics accuse him of being too concerned with personal credit and publicity.

Below: US infantry, including one armed with a bazooka antitank weapon, wait to go ashore on an assault landing.

Following the dreadful defeat at Stalingrad in the winter of 1942-43, the Nazis began for the first time to mobilise the total resources of their nation for war. The campaign was led by Propaganda Minister Goebbels, seen her in portrait and addressing a 'total war' rally.

Above left: Marshal Stalin, President Roosevelt and Prime Minister Churchill had their first meeting at Teheran in November 1943. The two Western Allies confirmed that they aimed to invade France in May 1944 and also to attack southern France around the same time.

Above: Among the previous meetings between Churchill and Roosevelt had been the Quebec conference in August 1943. Also present for this photograph were Prime Minister Mackenzie King of Canada (behind Roosevelt) and British Foreign Secretary Eden (front left).

Above right: US Chief of Staff General Marshall (right) with Eisenhower at Ike's HQ in North Africa in mid 1943.

Below left: Allied priorities for the Pacific theater were almost exclusively set by the American leaders. The two principal commanders were Admiral Nimitz of the US Pacific Fleet and General MacArthur in the Southwest Pacific area. Here Nimitz gives a briefing while MacArthur and the President look on. Nearest Nimitz is Admiral Leahy, the President's Chief of Staff.

Right: General Wingate had led operations behind Japanese lines in Burma in the early months of 1943. One of the decisions taken at the Quebec conference was to mount a second of these so-called Chindit operations in 1944.

US
US

1944

Throughout 1944 there was little respite from incessant Allied attacks by land, air and sea for either the Germans or the Japanese.

The best known campaign, of course, was the Allied invasion of France from D-Day on 6 June. Once ashore the Allied armies had to fight hard to break out from Normandy in June and July but then most of France was quickly liberated. Even while the fiercest fighting in Normandy was going on, the Soviets were engaged in Belorussia in an offensive which their historians correctly describe as the 'destruction of (the German) Army Group Center'. These summer months also brought Allied success in Italy where Rome fell two days before D-Day.

In the Pacific the pattern was very similar. MacArthur's forces advanced steadily along the northern coast of New Guinea and Nimitz's from island group to island group across the central Pacific. The capture of the Marianas in June-August gave the US bombers bases from which to attack the Japanese Home Islands and Japanese efforts to defend the Marianas resulted in a catastrophic naval defeat in the 'Great Marianas Turkey Shoot' (more properly the Battle of the Philippine Sea) which finally crippled Japan's naval air arm. Nimitz's and MacArthur's forces were then combined for the reconquest of the Philippines which began at Leyte in October. The Japanese again made a daring naval attack, relying on their surface forces, and this nearly achieved an imporant success because of poor American leadership. The chance was lost, however, and the only continuing significant threat to the Allied naval forces were the kamikaze or suicide attacks which were also begun at this time.

In Burma the Japanese mounted a major offensive in March with grandiose plans to march into India. They did encircle important British positions at Imphal and Kohima for a time but by the onset of the monsoon in July both had been completely relieved and the Japanese had fallen back in disarray after their army's worst defeat to date.

In Europe the German forces were still capable of achieving local successes at the end of the year as their attack in the Battle of the Bulge showed but the deeper reality was that Germany's allies were surrendering one by one (Finland, Rumania, Bulgaria, and Hungary all gave in in September-October), the Luftwaffe was now virtually impotent following in particular its catastrophic losses to the Americans in February and March, and Germany's armies, though substantial, were governed still more closely by the will of their Führer who had become still less rational and stable following the injuries he received in the abortive attempt on his life in July.

Left: Generals Matthew Ridgway (left) and James Gavin. Both commanded paratroop forces in the campaign in France and Belgium.

Right: 105mm howitzers of the 598th Field Artillery fire on enemy positions across the Arno River, Italy, August 1944. The 598th was a black unit in what was still a racially segregated US Army.

Previous page: This picture gives an excellent impression of the enormous number of transports and other ships and the great mass of supplies involved in the D-Day landings.

LOU II
413410
C
F2
S
413926

Above: General Ira Eaker (left) and General Carl Spaatz seen in London in early 1944. At that time Spaatz had just been promoted to command all US Strategic Bomber Forces involved in the attacks on Germany while Eaker led the Allied Air Forces in the Mediterranean Theater. Both men were forceful advocates of the importance of the strategic bombing operations.

Above left: Three P-51D Mustangs and a P-51C of the 8th Air Force's 361st Fighter Group pictured en route to Germany in the summer of 1944. The aircraft are flying in a somewhat closed-up version of the 'finger four' formation which had become standard for fighter operations by this stage in the war.

Far left: The bombardier of a B-17 Flying Fortress checks his plexiglass for any flaws or dirt that might hinder visibility in action. The aircraft is a later model B-17 fitted with the chin turret shown which experience proved to be necessary to defend against frontal attacks.

Left: Princess Elizabeth (as Her Majesty the Queen was then) performs the naming ceremony for a Flying Fortress 'Rose of York' at an English base.

Right: A V-2 rocket blasts off the launch pad. Over 3000 of these weapons were launched by the Germans in the course of the war, about one third of them against Britain. These attacks killed some 2700 people beginning in September 1944 and ending in March 1945.

Above: The 10-man crew of a Liberator bomber seen around their aircraft before a mission.

Left: Colonel Don Blakeslee, one of the top USAF aces, in the cockpit of his Mustang.

Above right: Mechanics at work on the Merlin engine of a Mustang fighter. It was the replacement of the earlier types of engine used in the first Mustangs by Merlins which transformed the Mustang's previously modest performance and made it a world beater.

Right: A camouflaged P-51 Mustang in flight over England.

2106950
WR
P

AB
2100686
AA
2100685

Left: British, Gurkha and West African members of the second Chindit expedition wait to be flown behind the Japanese lines.

Above right: The crew of a Bren gun carrier take a break overlooking the Ukhrul-Imphal road. This was the route which the relieving force took to Imphal.

Above: Admiral Lord Mountbatten, Allied Commander in Chief, South East Asia, talking to men of the US 1st Air Commando.

Below: Air transport played a vital role in the Burma campaign but older methods were also important. Here mules for local supply operations are being flown in to Imphal.

Left: The relieving force finally links up with the Imphal garrison on 22 June 1944.

Below: General Slim (left), his wife, and General Scoones, one of Slim's corps commanders.

Right: US and Chinese forces operated on the inland flank of the British forces in Burma. One of their most notable exploits was the capture of Myitkyina airfield in the summer of 1944. The airfield control tower is shown.

Below: The devastation after the fighting at Kohima. The area shown is the tennis court beside a local government officer's residence which became one of the focal points for the close-range battle.

MYITKYINA
NORTH AIRFIELD
CONS. BY 1888 INGR AVN BN
10TH U.S. ARMY AIR FORCE

MESSAGE
CENTER

Far top left: Several ploys were used to avoid compromising radio communication security. Attached to a US Marine artillery regiment somewhere in the South Pacific, these Navajo Indians relayed orders over field radio in their native tongue.

Top left: Generals Holland Smith (left) and Julian C Smith inspect wrecked Japanese installations on an island in the Gilbert group, February 1944. The conquest of the Marshall Islands was to form the first phase of the American counter-offensive in the Central Pacific, converging on the Mariana Islands under Admiral Nimitz's direction.

Left: US infantry and armor advance under cover of the smoke of pre-invasion shelling of Kwajalein.

Top: From left to right: Admiral Raymond A Spruance, unidentified, James V Forrestal (Secretary of the Navy), Major General Harry Schmidt, Major General H M Smith, Admiral Richard L Connolly, Colonel Evans F Carlson, Admiral C A Pownall.

Top right: Medical assistance in the field was often rendered under inhospitable conditions.

Above: Tanks of the US 7th Division advance on Kwajalein with infantry support.

Left: The scale of devastation rendered by the US naval shelling is evident in this view of Kwajalein Island after its capture, February 1944.

Bottom left: A Japanese Nakajima B5N Kate three-seat torpedo bomber falls victim to defensive fire from its intended victim, a US carrier.

Above: The submarine USS *Tinosa* berths at Pearl Harbor after returning from a war patrol, 1944. US submarines took a very heavy toll of Japanese shipping in 1944-45, preventing Japan from gaining any benefit from the resources of the large captured territories she still controlled.

Above right: US sea power was the key to their successful trans-Pacific drive that ended at the Japanese homeland. The battleship USS *Iowa* is pictured in 1944.

Right: Marines await the order to disembark from their LVT, on station off the beach at Roi, one of the five Marshall Islands captured in January-February 1944.

Left: Screen star (then Lieutenant) Clark Gable exchanges film roles for belts of machine gun ammunition at a Florida USAF Gunnery School.

Right: World light heavyweight champions Billy Conn of the US Army Air Service Command (right) and Freddie Mills of the RAF square up under the approving eye of a third pre-war boxing giant, Commander Jack Dempsey of the US Coast Guard (center).

Below: Bing Crosby does his bit for the war effort, singing to the US Air Force's 381st Bomb Group in the UK, September 1944.

Left: King George VI visited the major theaters of the European war. Accompanied by General Eisenhower, he here leaves the US headquarters during his visit to the American sector in France.

Below: The Normandy landings saw a veritable armada of sea power assembled to pour in supplies and reinforcements for the land campaign. The monitor HMS *Erebus* is pictured. This type of ship mounted very heavy guns and specialised in shore bombardment.

Right: Eisenhower boosts morale in the build-up to D-Day as British-based US paratroops prepare to play their part in the airborne assault.

23

Above: The guns belch fire as HMS *Glasgow* (foreground) and USS *Quincy* take up station off Cherbourg. Radar antennae have been painted out by the wartime censor.

Left: A GI's-eye view from an LCVP heading for Omaha Beach on D-Day. Each such landing craft could carry 36 soldiers, one vehicle or five tons of cargo.

Above right: Preparations for D-Day dated back to 1943. By the time of Exercise Fabius, mounted near Southampton, detailed plans for the most crucial Allied operation of the war in Europe had already been laid down.

Below: US landing craft mass off the Normandy beaches as the D-Day offensive gathers momentum.

RC
RC

49 51
R SEINE
VERNON
BRIDGE
8
115/LCT/4

Left: Bren gun carriers cross a hastily erected bridge across the Seine as the Allies broke out from Normandy and pushed eastwards towards Paris after the failure of the Germans to hold the Falaise Gap.

Right: This Sherman tank with 17-pounder gun waits ready for action by the side of a lane, June 1944. The Allies made slow work of advancing from the D-Day beachheads, but British attempts to occupy Caen proved successful in early July.

Below: British troops and vehicles on a D-Day beach. The tank at left is a Churchill AVRE, the special variant of the Churchill tank designed specifically to assist in the breaching of the Atlantic Wall.

3
64

Above: A German soldier attempts to defend Caen with his formidable MG42 weapon.

Left: A Churchill AVRE (left) and a stream of Bren Gun carriers in a captured French village.

Right: The damage and destruction suffered by the German Seventh Army in the Falaise Pocket.

Below: Churchill tanks of 31 Tank Brigade move into action.

Left: Members of the French Forces of the Interior – the Maquis – in their camp in the Breton woods.

Bottom left: A young German SS trooper (probably a member of 12th SS Pz Div 'Hitlerjugend') surrenders to the Allies as they push on into France.

Right: A US Army corporal distributes mail near St Lô, 27 July 1944.

Far right: Three of Britain's top soldiers in Normandy, from left, Generals Crocker, Dempsey and Bucknall. Dempsey commanded British Second Army, Crocker led I Corps, which became part of Canadian First Army and Bucknall led XXX Corps in Second Army.

Below: A pair of once-mighty Panzers stand forlorn and abandoned as the Germans continue their retreat through the Mortain-Falaise Gap.

Above left: General Jacques Philippe Leclerc (with cane), Commander of the French 2nd Armored Division, stands at the foot of the Arc de Triomphe during the celebration in Paris following the liberation of the French captial on 25 August 1944.

Above: British Special Service commandos advance through a French village.

Left: The end of the war for one German soldier.

Right: An Allied infantry patrol passing an abandoned German Mk IV tank.

Left: New Zealand machine gunners and range finder in action against Monastery Hill, the 435-meter high key position in the German defense of Cassino.

Below: 2,500 tons of bombs rain down on Monte Cassino in March 1944. It took the Allies over four months to conquer the area and secure the road to Rome in the face of spirited German resistance.

Right: Troops of the 92nd Division, Fifth Army, start scaling the steep muddy bank of the River Arno toward German positions in the Pontederra area, January 1944.

Above: A British 17-pdr antitank gun in action against German machine gun positions on Monastery Hill, near Cassino.

Left: A German shell halts the advance of Allied amphibious trucks landing supplies at Anzio.

Top right: The Supreme Allied Commander, Mediterranean Theater, General Sir Henry Maitland Wilson, discusses the battle situation with Commander of the Eighth Army Lieutenant General Sir Oliver Leese at Mignano, Italy in April 1944. The car carries a Polish flag because exiled Polish troops fought with the Allied forces.

Far top right: The Commander-in-Chief Allied Armies in Italy, General Sir Harold Alexander, pictured at his headquarters in Caserta, Italy.

Right: Allied tanks fitted with multi-barrel rocket launchers await the order to move forward.

AF

34

4·2 MOR HE
C174
C174

Left: A 4.2 inch heavy mortar of the Eighth Army in typically noisy action during the Allied assault on the Gustav Line.

Bottom left: A stunning aerial view of the monastery of St Benedict at Monte Cassino. Though the monastery was badly damaged, the Germans held firm in deep bunkers and were eventually outflanked by the Polish Corps.

Right: A column of German LSSAH vehicles pictured outside Milan.

Below: Sappers of the British 78th Division work on a Bailey bridge and a parallel track for tanks over the River Gari, Italy.

Left: A Churchill tank, possibly of 51st Royal Tank Regiment, is given a final check in a harbor area in Italy, July 1944.

Bottom left: 'Berlin or Bust' reads the legend on this American armored car.

Right: A British Bren gunner takes aim atop the rubble at Cassino. As well as the cultural damage done by the bombardment of this historic site, the destruction was also counterproductive militarily as the demolished buildings provided good defensive positions to the Germans.

Below right: The Allied view of Cassino, looking towards Monastery Hill, the immensely strong position dominating the Liri and Rapido Valleys at the Western end of the German Gustav Line that divided Italy.

Left: The US Marines deploy a captured Japanese mountain gun during the attack on Garapan, the administrative center of Saipan island, June 1944. The capture of the strategically important Marshall Islands – Saipan, Tinian and Guam – would effectively cut off Japan from the Philippines and Southeast Asia.

Below: Marines crawl under enemy fire to their assigned positions on the beach at Saipan. The Marine closest to camera swam ashore when his landing craft was hit by Japanese mortar fire. In the background are armored 'Buffalos' which supported the Marines in their invasion of the Marianas.

Right: Early on 26 June 1944 about 150 Japanese surrounded the 804th Engineer Area on three sides immediately adjoining Aslito Airfield on Saipan. In a pitched battle that lasted for several hours, the Japanese force was routed: here, men of the Counter Intelligence Corps unit examine a dead adversary, searching for any information of importance.

Bottom right: US Marines launch a hand grenade offensive against a nest of defending Japanese on Saipan.

Left: Two Marines take cover in a shell hole, June 1944. Japanese land resistance on Saipan was considerable, despite the losses inflicted on the Japanese First Mobile Fleet, the one-sided air battle passing into legend as 'the Great Marianas Turkey Shoot.'

Top right: Admiral Spruance (left) and General Holland Smith oversee the Saipan invasion.

Right: A Navy Corpsman attached to a Marine unit on Saipan administers a transfusion to a wounded Marine while another awaits treatment.

Below: US Marines of the 5th Amphibious Corps use a tank as a shield as they come ashore on Saipan.

Left: A pair of Mitsubishi A6M Zero fighters of No. 261 Navy Air Group, captured by invading US forces on Saipan in June 1944. 340 pilots and two carriers were lost by the Japanese in the Battle of the Philippine Sea.

Below: USS *Yorktown* as seen from fellow carrier USS *Wasp* in the Pacific, December 1944.

Far left: Germany mobilises its civilians in a last desperate attempt to stem the Allied advance, Berlin, November 1944.

Left: German armor in Budapest, summer 1944.

Below: A mixed German column of horse-drawn and motor vehicles on the retreat. The most difficult times for movement on the Eastern Front were just before and just after the harshest winter weather when the alternating nighttime freezes and daytime thaws helped generate deep and clinging mud as shown here.

Far left: Soviet T-34 tanks moving up for the attack on the Third Belorussian Front, 1944. A formidable fighting vehicle, the T-34 carried 76.2mm armament, weighed 25 tons and was protected by armor plate up to 45mm thick.

Left: A Tiger II crew in Budapest, 1944. The defeat of the Central Powers in 1918 had led to Hungary losing portions of territory, leaving it in sympathy with Italy and Germany.

Below: Luftwaffe men at work around a Heinkel 111 bomber on a frozen Russian airfield.

Left: A Luftwaffe Focke-Wulf Fw190G-3 in flight over Rumania in 1944.

Below: German infantrymen crowd round a Ju52 transport aircraft at an airfield in southern Russia in the summer of 1944.

Right: SS-General von dem Bach-Zelewski accepts the surrender of General Bor-Komorowski, leader of the Polish resistance, in November 1944.

Far right: General Vatutin, Commander of the 1st Ukranian Front, pictured in November 1943. His forces pushed south to retake the Ukraine, latterly under the command of General Zhukov who took over from April 1944.

Bottom right: Infantrymen and T-34 tanks on the Eastern Front.

46

Below: An Allied convoy makes its way through Belgium during the Allied advance to Antwerp.

Left: Hitler and Mussolini view the devastation caused by a failed assassination attempt – a bomb that exploded in the Führer's Conference Room, 20 July 1944.

Right: The people of Brussels welcome liberating British and Belgian troops as they enter the city on 3 September 1944. The next objectives for British and Canadian forces were river crossings leading into the Netherlands and Germany itself.

Far right: The Siegfried Line, Germany's once much-vaunted 'impregnable' defense, is breached on 15 September 1944 by the US 3rd Armored Division.

Top left: Troop-carrying gliders fill the fields of Holland as the great Allied airborne invasion gathers pace.

Left: A crack German Panzer unit in retreat as the Allied advance pinned them back to the Benelux border.

Above: British airborne forces ran into trouble at Arnhem, where 1st Airborne Division were dropped too far from the bridge that was their objective in a strongly defended area.

Right: Men of the 1st Paratroop Battalion take cover in a shell hole during 'Operation Market Garden', 17 September 1944.

Top left: British airborne troops move forward into Arnhem with their guns and equipment, 19 September 1944.

Bottom left: Advancing across Europe at speed put Allied logistics high on the priority agenda. Fuel dumps like this one played a vital role in facilitating rapid and continuous progress.

Above: A German StuG III assault gun dons protective camouflage during the Ardennes Offensive, November/December 1944. Intended to split US and British forces, this audacious campaign achieved the benefit of surprise and caused the Allies major problems.

Right: General Dwight D Eisenhower, Supreme Allied Commander, takes time for coffee during a visit to the divisional command post of the US 8th Infantry Division, 9 November 1944.

Z
Malmedy 13 km
St. Vith 8

Top left: An amphibious vehicle of the 2nd Panzer Grenadier Regiment near Recht, 17 December 1944. Kampfgruppe Peiper (also part of the 1st SS Panzer Division) was responsible for the massacre of US prisoners-of-war further north at Malmedy on the same day.

Bottom left: German armor moves into position as the 6th Panzer Army under Dietrich attempts to avoid being pushed back to the Rhine.

Above: US General MacAuliffe led the forces cut off in the town of Bastogne by the German advance. He brusquely refused a German request to surrender and inspired his men to hold out successfully until relief arrived.

Top right: US soldiers cautiously approach a war-torn home in Wiltz, Luxembourg, as they search for hidden Germans.

Right: A US infantryman from the 26th Division eats cold rations in the snow somewhere on the Western Front, December 1944.

Left: The 740-vessel Leyte invasion fleet gathers for the October landings. The fleet, which included 17 aircraft carriers, was the first target for Japan's Kamikaze (or 'Divine Wind') suicide attacks, three US carriers being hit on 25th October.

Right: Although the Japanese cruiser *Kumano* sustained major damage in this October 1944 attack by US Navy bombers following the battle off Samar, she stayed afloat until the next month.

Below: Two US Navy torpedo boats come under attack in Leyte Gulf. At Leyte, the twofold American offensive of MacArthur and Nimitz came together, while the hammer blow dealt to the Imperial Japanese Navy put the writing on the wall.

Below: US escort carriers and their supports come under fire during a sustained two and one half-hour attack by the Japanese fleet off Leyte Gulf. Despite three Japanese forces being involved, the eventual outcome of the sea battles was a comprehensive US victory.

Bottom left: US Medium Landing Ships approach the beach during the Leyte landings, 20 October 1944. General Walter Krueger's Sixth Army outnumbered the Japanese defenders by 130,000 to 20,000 and predictably won a comprehensive victory on land.

Bottom, center: Activities aboard a US Navy torpedo boat preparing for the Battle of Surigao Strait, 24 October 1944, in which the US Seventh Fleet under Kinkaid destroyed Nishimura's Force C in a night battle.

Bottom right: HMAS *Australia*'s damaged smokestack bears witness to the intensity of the fighting. *Australia* is believed to have been the first Allied ship hit by a Kamikaze aircraft.

Left: The Japanese Force A including the giant battleship *Musashi* which was sunk, under concerted US air attack during the Battle of the Sibuyan Sea, 24 October 1944.

Right: The damaged aircraft carrier *Princeton* with its complement of torpedo bombers clearly visible, receives assistance from the cruiser USS *Birmingham*.

Below: USS *Heermann* (DD-532) laying smoke early in the action off Samar, 25 October 1944, in which Kurita's Force A was repulsed by the US Seventh Fleet.

LUCKY
LEGS II

Left: A US tank moves forward on Bougainville in the Solomon Islands, infantrymen following in its cover to mop-up Japanese infiltrators behind the lines.

Bottom left: American paratroops of the 503rd Parachute Infantry land on Kamiri Strip on Noemfoor Island, July 1944.

Right: Vice Admiral Thomas C Kinkaid (left), Commander of Allied Naval Forces in SWPA and General Douglas MacArthur on the flag bridge of the USS *Phoenix* during bombardment of Los Negros Island, 28 February 1944.

Below: USS *England* (DE-635) off San Francisco, 9 February 1944. The *England* established a unique record in May 1944 when, in a period of less than two weeks, she sank six Japanese submarines in operations off New Guinea.

330
335
335

Left: Troops unload ammunition from LCTs at Rendova Island, New Georgia. The New Georgia campaign began with landings at the end of June 1943.

Top right: Aerial view of Middleburg Island, off the coast of Dutch New Guinea, shortly after the 836th Aviation Engineers started work on the airstrip, August 1944. The end of the previous year had seen the Japanese driven from the island by the US advance.

Right: Aerial view of a phase of construction on Mar Strip near Cape Sansapor on the Dutch New Guinea mainland, August 1944. Trees have been cleared and grading of the strip is in progress; little work has been done on the taxiways and revetments as yet.

Below: After the preliminary clearing was made on Middleburg Island, off the coast of Dutch New Guinea, bulldozers, graders and scrapers followed the crews clearing the jungle. By this time other units had landed, installed and tested radar defense and anti-aircraft positions, August 1944.

1945

1945 was the year in which the war was won.

Despite their recent brief setback in the Ardennes, the Western Allies began the year pushing steadily into Germany, would cross the Rhine in March and eventually link up with the Soviet forces at Torgau on the Elbe on 25 April. For their part the Soviets had rolled remorselessly across Poland and eastern Germany in the first months of the year before fighting their way into Berlin in a vicious battle in the second half of April.

Hitler continued to urge Germany to fight on, growing less and less in touch with reality day by day. He finally committed suicide on 30 April with the Soviet forces only yards from his bunker and his thousand year Reich did not long survive him. Britain and the US were able to celebrate V-E Day (Victory in Europe) on 8 May. We can now see that the reconquest of the two halves of Europe by armies espousing different political systems would govern two different approaches to the rebuilding of the continent's political and economic institutions but in May 1945 that, like the unfinished business of the punishment of war crimes and other matters, was a problem for the future.

In the Pacific the Allies continued to close in on Japan. All the time they were doing so they were also destroying Japan's capacity to make war by the very successful submarine campaign against her shipping and by the devastating bombing of her cities. In Burma the British inflicted a further series of major defeats on the Japanese and had recaptured the whole country by May. In the Philippines new landings were made on Luzon, the principal island of the group, in January and by March most of this island was in American hands also.

The US Marines captured the tiny stepping-stone island of Iwo Jima at great cost in February and the last stage before the planned invasion of the Japanese Home Islands was the bloody capture of Okinawa in April-June.

On 16 July 1945 a new element entered military and international affairs when the first atomic bomb was tested by the Americans at Alamagordo in New Mexico. President Truman (Roosevelt had died in April) decided that the atom bomb should be dropped on Japan in an attempt to end the war without the enormous Allied and Japanese casualties anticipated if the invasion of Japan itself was to be carried out. Hiroshima on 6 August and Nagasaki on the 9th were the targets for the two attacks. On 8 August Stalin kept his promise to the US and Britain from earlier in the war and declared war on Japan. Soviet forces were very quickly smashing through the Japanese in Manchuria. Whether because of these defeats or the atom bomb attacks has been debated ever since, but the Japanese quickly capitulated. World War II ended with the signing of the Japanese surrender aboard the USS *Missouri* in Tokyo Bay on 2 September 1945.

Previous page: B-17s of the 91st Bomb Group of the Eighth Air Force at 24,000 feet en route to Oberpfaffenhofen, Germany.

Right: A concentration camp inmate, rescued by the Allies, but perhaps too weak to survive. Such scenes rightly shocked the world.

Below left: US infantrymen fire on Japanese positions in the fiercely-defended Intramuros area of Manila in January 1945.

Below: Men of an RAF bomber squadron celebrate around one of their Lancaster aircraft.

Above: General Douglas MacArthur watches from a balcony window and a crowd of soldiers look on as a small group of Japanese soldiers surrender in Manila. MacArthur's promise, in the dark days of 1942, that he would return to the Philippines had been triumphantly fulfilled.

Left: Men of the 32nd Infantry Division in good heart at a soldiers' show on Luzon, the northernmost island of the Philippines in August 1945.

Top right: The US Army reoccupies Clark Field near Manila, as Japanese gun emplacements (background) sustain a direct hit.

Right: The final assault on Manila's last Japanese stronghold, the walled city of Intramuros, was delivered from the steps of the city's Post Office. Here men of the US 145th Infantry are seen in front of the Post Office building.

Above: Two platoons of American infantry fight their way along the Old Burma Road, reopened in January 1945 as the Japanese were pushed back in north Burma.

Left: Admiral Lord Louis Mountbatten, Supreme Allied Commander, Southeast Asia Theater, (left), visits General Douglas MacArthur, during his stopover in Manila, July 1945.

Top right: A scout car and a Sherman tank disembark from a makeshift barge on the Eastern bank of the Irrawaddy, February 1945, as the Allies advanced to engage the retreating Japanese forces.

Right: The outskirts of Pegu, 50 miles north of Rangoon, burn as the Fourteenth Army's Shermans roll southward to secure victory for General Sir William Slim.

202
202

Far left: An American landing craft damaged during the invasion of Iwo Jima.

Left: An airborne view of Iwo Jima from a 7th Air Force B-24 Liberator bomber, one of many sent to attack the strategically important – just eight square miles in size – island prior to the US landing.

Below: The soft, volcanic ash of the beach on Iwo Jima hampered the American landing effort, as the abandoned jeep clearly shows.

Right: Marine Corps personnel attend a briefing immediately prior to the Iwo Jima invasion.

Left: Vice-Admiral Richard Kelly Turner (left) with Major General Harry Schmidt and Lieutenant General Holland M Smith (right), the trio who directed operations against Iwo Jima.

Bottom left: Turner and Holland Smith survey the action at first hand.

Right: An observer on Iwo Jima locates an enemy machine gun emplacement on a map with a view to Allied artillery destroying it.

Below: The Second Battalion, 27th US Marines land on Iwo Jima, 19 February 1945. Two Marine divisions had landed by the time the Japanese opened their fire, hoping to make the invaders believe they would encounter no resistance but opening fire fatal minutes too late.

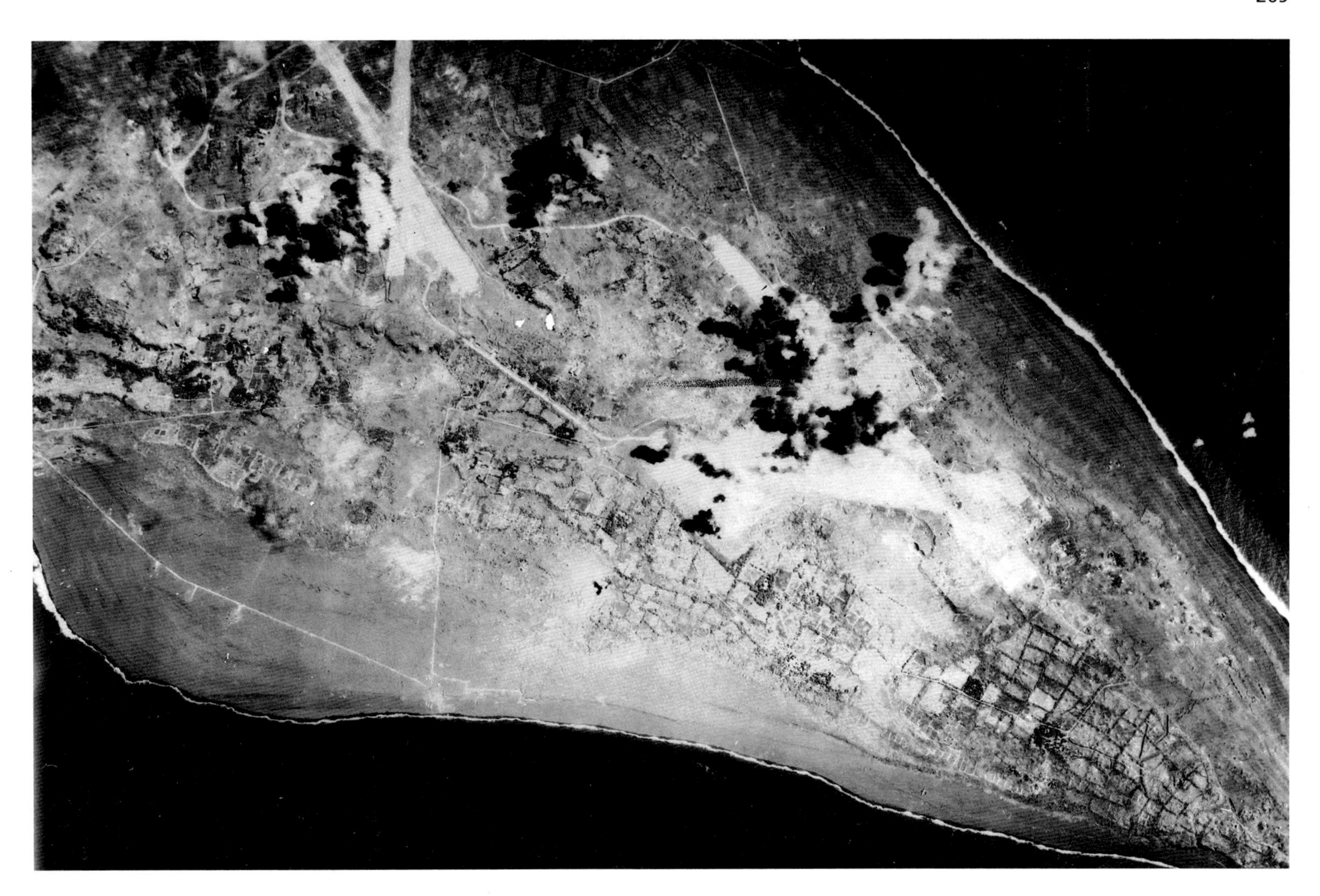

Top left: The smoke of battle obscures Mount Suribachi, the massif at the island's southernmost tip and the goal of the 5th Division, US Marine Corps as they work their way uphill from Red Beach . The mountain was secured after three costly days of combat.

Left: Marines with flamethrowers work their way towards Iwo Jima's Mount Suribachi. The US flag was raised on the summit on 23rd February, but major Japanese resistance on the island continued for a further three days.

Above: An aerial view of Iwo Jima, its airstrips (left and right) targeted by bombs of the 7th US Army Air Force. The cluster of bombs center hit gun emplacements.

Right: Despite withering Japanese small-arms fire, Marines establish a landline for field telephone communications with the front line.

Right: An amphibious tractor loaded with US Marines leaves an LST. Skill in amphibious operations was a key to US success in the inexorable advance towards the Japanese homeland.

Left: Marines blast Japanese positions near the base of Mount Suribachi. Landing on the south coast of the rocky island, US forces compressed the Japanese into the north-east corner where a network of underground defenses aided concealment.

Below: Marines go ashore at Iwo Jima. Hand-to-hand combat for control of the island cost the lives of nearly 7000 US servicemen: the 22,000 Japanese defenders were killed almost to a man.

954 H 05
10

Left: An American DUKW 'waddles' into the Rhine for the crossing to the east bank. An ever increasing flow of men and material forges across the river, pouring into the rapidly expanding bridgehead.

Right: British soldiers advance with caution as their sector of the Allied front reached the Rhine in March 1945.

Below: In inhospitable winter conditions, American troops of the 9th Armored Division prepare to tow away Sherman tanks knocked out by the German drive near Bastogne, Belgium.

Left: Troops of a Scottish division leave their assault craft after crossing the Rhine. The drive from the Rhine to the Elbe was to meet pockets of determined German opposition.

Above: Two German soldiers captured by troops of the Third US Army on the outskirts of Margorette, Belgium, under military police guard.

Right: The capture, intact, of the Ludendorff rail bridge over the Rhine at Remagen by the US First Army on 7 March 1945 was the single most important Allied move in crossing the greatest water obstacle in Western Europe.

Below: British troops prepare boats and other bridging equipment for the Rhine crossings in their sector.

Left: The Allied advance through Belgium into Germany was achieved in the face of not only the enemy but the weather. A British 17-pdr SP ploughs through the water on the Krahenburg Road.

Right: German high-ranking officers surrender at Field Marshal Montgomery's HQ on Luneberg Heath, 4 May 1945.

Far right: The German delegates have a conference among the trees.

Below: An American antiaircraft position on the banks of the Rhine.

Top left: The American generals who helped pave the way to victory in Europe are pictured on 11 May 1945, four days after the formal cessation of hostilities, at 12th Army Group Headquarters, Bad Wildungen, Germany. Seated in the front row, left to right: General Simpson, US Ninth Army; General Patton, US Third Army; General Spaatz, USATAF; General Eisenhower, Supreme Allied Commander; General Bradley, 11th Army Group; General Hodges, US First Army and General Gerow, US Fifteenth Army.

Bottom left: The railway viaduct at Bielefeld photographed three days after the attack by RAF Bomber Command on 14th March 1945. The huge size of craters caused by 12,000lb and 22,000lb bombs can be seen when compared with the house at the bottom of the frame.

Right: SS troops under British guard load trucks with bodies from Belsen for transporting to burial grounds.

Below: The bodies of Mussolini, his mistress and other associates hang upside down after being shot by partisans in April 1945.

Top left: Nazi Field Marshal Gerd von Rundstedt, former German supreme commander on the Western Front, stands with his son, Leutnant Hans von Runstedt, and a German medical attendant (right) following his capture by troops of the 36th Division, Seventh US Army, at Bad Toelz, south of Munich, Germany. Von Rundstedt was receiving treatment for arthritis in a hospital in Bad Toelz when captured on 3 May. Put in charge of 'Fortress Europe' in the spring of 1944, von Rundstedt later led the retreat back into the Reich. Following the failure of the German Ardennes offensive, he was replaced by Field Marshal Kesselring in March 1945.

Above: The Soviet Guards Cavalry Corps meet units of the Third US Army on the Elbe, May 1945. Although it is likely the western Allies could have reached Berlin and Prague in the previous month, the US had pledged to the Soviets that the advance would stop at the Elbe.

Left: A street in the Karlsruhe area is renamed courtesy of a zealous American soldier, December 1944.

Right: A copy of the historic Unconditional Surrender Document signed by the German officers in Field Marshal Montgomery's tent. Note the change in the date, initialled by Montgomery.

Instrument of Surrender

of

All German armed forces in HOLLAND, in

northwest Germany including all islands,

and in DENMARK.

1. The German Command agrees to the surrender of all German armed forces in HOLLAND, in northwest GERMANY including the FRISIAN ISLANDS and HELIGOLAND and all other islands, in SCHLESWIG-HOLSTEIN, and in DENMARK, to the C.-in-C. 21 Army Group. This to include all naval ships in these areas. These forces to lay down their arms and to surrender unconditionally.

2. All hostilities on land, on sea, or in the air by German forces in the above areas to cease at 0800 hrs. British Double Summer Time on Saturday 5 May 1945.

3. The German command to carry out at once, and without argument or comment, all further orders that will be issued by the Allied Powers on any subject.

4. Disobedience of orders, or failure to comply with them, will be regarded as a breach of these surrender terms and will be dealt with by the Allied Powers in accordance with the accepted laws and usages of war.

5. This instrument of surrender is independent of, without prejudice to, and will be superseded by any general instrument of surrender imposed by or on behalf of the Allied Powers and applicable to Germany and the German armed forces as a whole.

6. This instrument of surrender is written in English and in German.

The English version is the authentic text.

7. The decision of the Allied Powers will be final if any doubt or dispute arises as to the meaning or interpretation of the surrender terms.

B. L. Montgomery
Field-Marshal

BLM
4 May 1945
1830 hrs

v. Friedeburg
Kinzel
G. Wagner
[illegible]
[illegible]

Top left: The Soviet army enters Berlin in May 1945 after one of the hardest-fought battles of the war. The city would be partitioned for 45 years.

Above: Fighting rages in the Berlin streets as Soviet armor moves in from north and south to meet across the Charlottenberg Chaussee.

Left: Powerful Soviet artillery shells enemy fortifications, Berlin, 1945.

Below: Soviet troops cross the Oder River, the last major natural barrier between them and Berlin.

Above: 16 year old William Hübner, one of the youngest Iron Cross recipients. By 1945 boys even younger than this were being drafted into military service in Germany.

Left: A Waffen-SS soldier with anti-tank weapon travels to the front.

Right: The fall of Berlin in early May was never more graphically depicted than by this photograph of Soviet troops raising their flag over the last bastion of the Reich.

PEGASUS V
74
X
T 188464
74
R
T 188888

Left: 10,000 men representing Britain's three fighting services march in triumph through the Charlottenberg Chaussee, 21 July 1945. Those present included Field Marshal Sir Henry Maitland-Wilson, Field Marshal Sir Harold Alexander, Admiral of the Fleet Sir Andrew Cunningham, Marshal of the Royal Air Force Sir Charles Portal, Field Marshal Sir Bernard Montgomery, Field Marshal Sir Alan Brooke and politicians Winston Churchill, Anthony Eden and Clement Attlee. Led by Brigadier J M K Spurling, DSO, the march past took 40 minutes to complete.

Bottom left: A battery of 'Katyusha' rocket mortars delivers a deadly salvo in the Carpathians, 1944.

Top right: An anti-tank missile is demonstrated to the German Home Guard in March 1945.

Right: A Wehrmacht armband identifies a member of the German Home Guard or Volkssturm.

Above: Marine F4U Corsair fighters are silhouetted against anti-aircraft tracers during a Japanese air raid on Yontan Airfield, Okinawa, in April 1945.

Left: Major General Lemuel C Shepherd, Jr, Commanding General of the 6th Marine Division, studies a map during the battle for Okinawa, April 1945.

Top right: Two US Marines armed with a Bazooka inch their way up a hill two miles north of the Okinawan capital, Naha.

Bottom right: The Japanese battleship *Yamato* is hit by a bomb during the Battle of Sibuyan Sea, 24 October 1944. The *Yamato* survived this engagement but was sunk by carrier planes during the Okinawa campaign. The *Yamato* was sent, effectively as a giant Kamikaze, to attack the US forces off Okinawa, without enough fuel aboard to make the return journey.

Left: One US Marine comforts another after witnessing the death of a comrade on an Okinawa hillside. These men took part in the bitter fighting waged against Shuri, the Japanese stronghold two miles east of Naha.

Below: US Marines deploy a 'Satchel' charge against a group of Japanese found in a cave. The destruction of the Japanese 32nd Army was achieved at an horrendous cost – over 8,000 men killed and nearly 32,000 wounded.

Top right: The carrier USS *Bunker Hill* (CV-17) sustains a hit. 36 US and British ships were lost at Okinawa, with hundreds more damaged.

Below right: The battleship USS *New Mexico* discharges her guns off Okinawa, April 1945. The invasion began on 1 April after a period of 'softening-up' with attacks from air and sea.

Below far right: A US Navy gun captain opening the breech of a 16-inch gun in a battleship's turret.

Left: The steeple of a Christian church below Shuri Castle on Okinawa provided a snipers' nest for the Japanese. The US Marines in the foreground are covering the building while a patrol comes in from the rear to neutralise it.

Bottom far left: A lone Marine stands in the wreckage of a theater building in Naha, May 1945.

Bottom left: A US Marine Corps photographer cleans the inside of the plexiglass nose of a P-38's belly tank, June 1945.

Right: The aftermath of a Kamikaze attack on HMS *Formidable*, stationed off Okinawa, on 4 May 1945. The British Pacific Fleet joined the main US forces for the Okinawa operations.

Below: US ships bombard Okinawa. The scale of losses sustained in the invasion lent weight to the argument for the use of the nuclear bomb to bring the war to a speedy conclusion.

Opposite left: One of USS *Alaska*'s Curtiss SC-1 float-planes moves up to the landing mat to be picked up by an aircraft crane. Air observation played an important part in tracking enemy ship movements.

Opposite right: Victory markings denoting Japanese planes downed are applied to a 5-inch gun director of a US destroyer.

Left: Vice-Admiral Marc Mitscher, commander of the US Task Force 58 that proved so successful in the Battle of the Philippine Sea.

Below: The radar picket destroyer *Aaron Ward* after being hit by five suicide planes during the Okinawa campaign. The radar picket ships operated some distance from the main Allied forces to give warning of attacks but often themselves became the Japanese targets.

MBS
CBS
NBC

Far left: Major General Curtis LeMay, who commanded the final stages of the strategic air operations against Japan.

Left: US President Harry Truman who, in July 1945, accepted his Chiefs of Staff's recommendation that Hiroshima – Japan's seventh largest city – should be the first target for the atomic bomb.

Bottom left: Boeing B-29s prepare to take off for Tokyo at one-minute intervals.

Top right: Incendiary bombs drop towards the dock area of Kobe, Japan's sixth largest city, as Marianas-based US B-29 Superfortresses drop 3000 tons of bombs and blast a ten-mile (16km) area extending along Osaka Bay, 4 June 1945.

Bottom right: Despite damage from anti-aircraft shell, a US B-29 Superfortress continues its bombing run over Osaka during an attack on Japan's largest industrial center on 1 June 1945.

Left: Soviet naval ratings of the Pacific Fleet hoist the Soviet flag over Port Arthur, 1945. The Soviets kept previous promises to join the war against Japan, declaring war on 8 August 1945. Their forces began an invasion of Manchuria the next day and some authorities believe that their rapid and overwhelming success did as much to make Japan surrender as the atom bomb attacks.

Below left: Colonel Paul Tibbetts with the B-29, named 'Enola Gay', he flew to bomb Hiroshima on 6 August 1945.

Below: Nagasaki was the second Japanese city to be subjected to atomic bomb attack, on 9 August 1945.

Top right and bottom right: The unparalleled destruction witnessed at Hiroshima and Nagasaki resulted in an estimated total of 131,000 immediate deaths plus many later and innumerable wounded.

Above: MacArthur signs the surrender document aboard the USS *Missouri* in Tokyo Bay on 2 September 1945, with Generals Wainwright and Percival watching. Both had just been freed from Japanese POW camps following their detention since respectively surrendering the Philippines and Malaya to the Japanese in 1942.

Above: High-ranking Allied officers board the USS *Missouri* for the formal signing ceremony that ended the war in the Far East.

Left: Lieutenant General Roy Geiger, Commanding General Fleet Marine Force, Pacific examines the card – signed by General MacArthur and Admirals Nimitz and Halsey – given to those who attended the surrender ceremony.

Right: The center of Hiroshima, Japan, obliterated by the first atomic bomb. The aiming point was the bridge, fourth from top in center. The harder, concrete structures were more resistant to the overpressure.

Bottom right: Japanese listen to news of the unconditional surrender, 15 August 1945. The decision was given in an unprecedented radio broadcast by Emperor Hirohito.

INDEX

Page numbers in *italics* refer to illustrations.

Acknowledgments

The publishers would like to thank Michael Heatley for his assistance in compiling the captions in this book; David Eldred who designed it and Ron Watson who compiled the index. The following agencies kindly supplied the illustrations on the pages noted.

Bison Picture Library pp 9 top, 14 top, 17 center, 18-19 (3), 24-25 (4), 26 top, 27 (3), 30 top two, 31, 34 top two, 38 top, 39 top, 47 top right, 50-51 (4), 54 bottom right, 55 both, 56-57, 58-59 (6), 62 top two, 71 top, 72-72 (5), 81 lower two, 89 top left, 92 top left, 114 both, 115, 118-119 (4), 144 top, 146 top right, 147, 158 top left, 159 both, 168 lower
Bundesarchiv pp 6-7, 10-11, 14 lower, 15 both, 16 both, 20-21 top three, 22 top & center, 23 top two, 26 bottom, 29 top left, 30 lower, 33 top, 34-35, 35, 37 lower left, 39 lower two, 45 both, 48 lower, 49 both, 54 top, 57 top two, 60 (3), 61 top, 62-63, 65 top two, 66 center, 88 both, 89 lower, 91 lower, 93, 94, 94-95, 97 lower, 98-99, 100 top, 114-115, 116 lower, 117 top, 120 top left, 131 both, 132 (3), 133 bottom, 143 top, 144 lower, 148 top, 149 top, 154 lower, 157 lower, 158-9, 161 lower, 182 (3), 185 both, 223 top, 232-233 (3), 234-235, 235, 236 both, 237 top left, 238 top, 240 lower, 244 both, 284 both, 287 both
Imperial War Museum, London pp 9 lower, 12, 13, 17 top, 20-21 lower, 22 bottom, 23 bottom, 28, 28-29, 29 top right, 32 (3) 33 lower, 36 (3), 37 top & right, 40-41 (5), 46 both, 47 top left & bottom, 48 top, 52-53 (5), 61 lower, 64 (3), 65 bottom, 66 top & bottom, 67 bottom, 70 (3), 70-71, 76, 77 lower, 79 both, 80 top, 81 top, 82 lower, 86-87 top three, 89 top right, 91 top, 92-93, 95 both, 96, 96-97, 97 top, 98 top, 99 top, 100 lower, 101 both, 102 top, 103 top left, 104 top, 133 top, 137 top, 139 lower, 151 lower, 152-153, 153 top left, 154 top, 155 top, 156 top, 157 both, 160 both, 163 both, 164 top, 178 lower, 181, 187 lower, 196-197 (4), 198-199 (4), 206 both, 208 top, 209 top, 210-211 (3), 212-213, 215 top right, 216 (3), 218 both, 220 top, 221 top two, 222 both, 223 lower, 224 top, 225 both, 239 top left, 240 top, 241 both, 247 top, 259 both, 263 both, 273, 274 top left, 274-275, 276-277 top three, 279 both, 281, 286 top, 293 top
Novosti Press Agency pp 18 lower, 44, 56 top, 116 top, 117 lower, 120 top right & below, 121 both, 141 both, 142 top, 142-143, 145 both, 146 top left, 146-147, 148 lower, 234, 237 top left & bottom, 282-283 (4), 285, 298, 298 top
RAF Museum, London pp 38 lower, 259 lower, 278 lower
US Army pp 67 top two, 78 lower, 80 lower, 82 top, 83 top, 102-103, 104 bottom, 130 both, 137 lower, 140 lower, 149 lower, 150 both, 152 top, 153 top right, 155 lower, 158 top right, 161 top, 164 lower, 165 both, 178 top two, 179 both, 180, 180-181, 184 both, 186 both, 187 top two, 190, 191, 207, 212 top, 213 top two, 214 both, 215 lower & top left, 217, 219, 220 lower, 221 lower, 224 lower, 238-239, 239 top right, 242 lower, 243 both, 245 (3), 252 both, 254, 258, 260-261 (4), 262 both, 272, 272-273, 274 top right, 275 top, 276-277 lower, 278 top, 280 (3), 301 both
US Air Force pp 78 top, 83 lower, 134-135, 138 both, 162, 162-163, 166-167 (4), 168 top, 176 lower, 183 lower, 192-193 (5), 194-195 (4), 204, 205 both, 255 (3), 256-257, 296-297 (5), 298 lower two, 299 both
US Marine Corps pp 126 lower, 127 lower, 128-129 (4), 136, 140 top, 170 both, 174-175 (4), 176 top, 177 top right & bottom, 200-201 (6), 203 bottom, 226-227 (4), 228-229 (4), 264-271 all, 288 both, 289 top, 290 both, 292 (3)
US Navy pp 42-43, 54 bottom left, 68-69 (4), 74-75, 77 top, 84 (3), 86-87 main pic, 90 both, 92 top right, 103 top right, 104 center, 105-112 all, 122-123 (4), 124-125 (3), 126 top, 127 top, 139 top, 151 top, 169 both, 171 both, 172-173 (5), 177 top left, 183 top, 188-189, 202 both, 203 top two, 208 center, 208-209, 230-231 both, 246-247 (3), 248-249 (4), 250-251 (3), 253 both, 289 lower, 291 both, 293 lower, 294-295 (4), 300 (3).